MIND OVER MUSIC

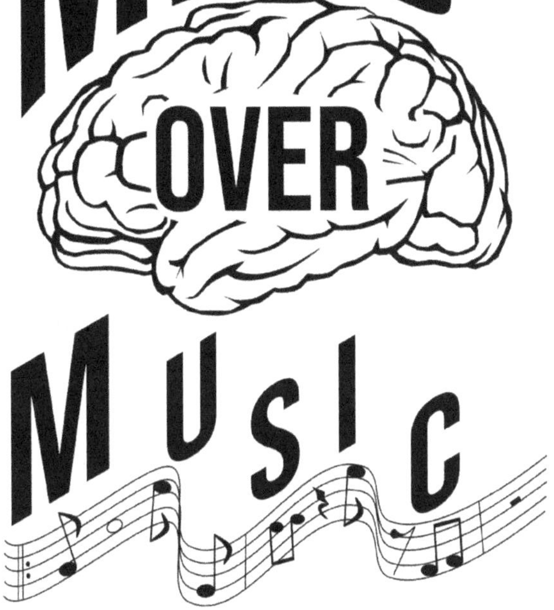

Break Through The Blocks To Get Into The Studio And On The Stage Today

By **Jaime Vendera**
Bestselling Author, *Raise Your Voice*
and *The Ultimate Breathing Workout*

With **Dr. Joe Vitale**
Bestselling Author, *The Awakened Millionaire*
and *Zero Limits*

Copyright © 2019 by Vendera Publishing

All rights reserved. No part of this book may be reproduced in any form, by any means, electronic or otherwise, including photocopying, scanning, downloading, or by any data storage system, without written permission from the publisher.

Interior Design: Daniel Middleton | www.scribefreelance.com
Cover Design: Molly Burnside | www.crosssidedesigns.com
Photography for Jaime Vendera: Daniel Baker Design
Photography for Joe Vitale: Brian Fitzsimmons
Editor: Richard Dalglish

ISBN: 978-1-936307-50-0 (Ingram Paperback)
ISBN: 978-1-936307-45-6 (Amazon Paperback)
ISBN: 978-1-936307-48-7 (eBook)

Published in the United of America

CONTENTS

Why Anything is Possible: An Introduction by Dr. Joe Vitale 5

Welcome to the Show 9

PART ONE: *The Tale of Two Artists* 15
    Chapter One: The Story of Jaime 17
    Chapter Two: The Story of Joe 22

PART TWO: *The Story of You* 33
    Chapter Three: Discovering the Origin of Your Musical Fire 35
    Chapter Four: Feeling the Fire 44
    Chapter Five: When the Fire Dims 48

PART THREE: *Fueling the Fire* 59
    Chapter Six: Setting Your First Goal
    (Step One—Setting Your Intention) 61
    Chapter Seven: Clearing the Path
    (Step Two—Clearing Negative Beliefs) 70
    Chapter Eight: Reaching the Finish Line
    (Step Three—Taking Action) 82
    Chapter Nine: Where's the Proof? 95

On With the Show 111

About Jaime Vendera 113

About Dr. Joe Vitale 114

WHY ANYTHING IS POSSIBLE

An Introduction by Dr. Joe Vitale

O NE DAY I CHECKED FACEBOOK and there was a curious message from Jaime Vendera. I knew Jaime from his books on singing, which helped me with my own vocal technique. I had gone from zero to musician in the span of a few years, and Jaime was one of my never-met coaches along the way. I had bought and read his books. I knew he was a badass vocal coach. His ideas had helped me, and still do. So I looked at his message. He wrote:

"Listen up, Vitale, the Universe smacked me again to put this in your brain ... and I am pretty sure I told you this a few years back :) You REALLY need to write an "LOA/Ramp up your music making mojo" type book. It's not a book about the art of songwriting, but more a book lining out the steps to get a musician off their butt and finishing their songs and recording/releasing them ... You are THE perfect person to write this considering what you've accomplished!!! If you don't write this, that voice in my head will never leave me alone. It will pester me to pester you until you hear it too;) There, I told you, just as I was instructed to do. So now please write the book so it will make the voices stop, hahahaha;)"

I admired his playful audacity. I've written over 70 books and Jaime knew it. He also knew my expertise in self-help methods, applied to would-be musicians, would be a hit. He also knew that my appearance in the movie *The Secret*, and my books on the Law of

Attraction (LOA), made me qualified to teach musicians. But I also felt that this idea was his, not mine. I suspected he was just tossing a monkey at me and hoping I'd adopt it. I already had enough monkeys. So I wrote back to him saying:

"Hmmmm ... Maybe it's in your head and not mine so you write it and I add to it to be coauthor ..."

Seemed like a fair counter offer to me. Jaime could blow me off but at least I didn't dismiss him. I was acknowledging his idea but turning it back in his direction. I was sending the monkey home. To my surprise, he accepted my challenge. He wrote back saying:

"Hahaha, well that will work then. I just had this image of you explaining how you knocked out so many songs so quick. I'm knocking out four new products right now but I'll start writing soon."

He did, too. Not only did he start writing, but he caught on fire and wrote the entire book by himself. A week later he wrote to me saying:

"Just letting you know I never back down from a challenge;) I am writing three new books, filming two new videos, two new audio programs, and writing/recording as we speak, and it is all part of the focus of this book. I feel it should be called MIND OVER MUSIC and show the musician that writer's block is only a state of mind, as well as teach them how to get it out of their heads and recorded in record time. So, I had a quick question for you: Do you have a musical bio I can copy/paste? I want to mention the day you decided to become a musician and record and ALL the albums you have released since then. I am blown away by your energy and what you've done. It is soooo refreshing."

He was referring to my becoming a musician with 15 albums recorded in about 5 years. That seemed impossible to most people. But I teach "Anything Is Possible" (and wrote a book titled that very statement). I sent him the material he wanted, and he inserted it into his book. Then I read the book. Now it was my turn to be blown away. He wrote the book with a passion I rarely see in other authors. And he gave steps and secrets and insights along the way. He included me and my story of becoming a musician, beginning with zero experience and going on to record albums, study with Melissa Etheridge, and even overcome terror to sing on stage with my band.

In short, he had created the very book he wanted me to write. And he did it without me. But being the kind and generous soul that he is, he wanted my name as coauthor because he said I inspired the entire project. He wanted me to have credit. That's the kind of loving soul he is. So I accepted.

The good news for you, the reader, is you get to benefit from the combined experience of two authors, teachers, coaches, and musicians: us. I'm living proof that you can dissolve blocks and get in the studio and on stage, no matter who you are, where you are, what your level of experience, your age, or much else. And Jaime is living proof that when you adopt his methods, you will shine in the studio and on stage.

All in all, you are about to read an illuminating guide to getting past the excuses and blocks and into the studio and onto the stage. Bright lights and applause await, as well as the deep satisfaction of sharing your music with the world.

And now, curtain up ...

—Dr. Joe Vitale
www.MrFire.com

WELCOME TO THE SHOW

S O, YOU WANNA BE A STAR???
Who doesn't?!?!?!
Who doesn't want to hear their music brought to life, take the stage, put on an awesome show, hear people singing your lyrics back to you and screaming your name, wowing the audience and pulling them into your story. I know I do!

As a vocal coach for over twenty years, I've had the pleasure of working with countless singers, including beginners and touring veterans alike, from the ages of seven past seventy. One of the most heartbreaking parts of working with musicians is all the stories of regret and failure I've heard over the years. There was a common thread among many of the stories I've been told, with the more common regrets starting with:

I missed my chance to make it big, and *I never got to perform like I dreamed*, and *I can never seem to finish my album*, and *I was always too afraid of what people thought of me.*

These are but a few of the thoughts my students shared with me.

However, not every student shared stories of regret. I've had many singers who had a goal in mind, paid no attention to what others thought of them, and took action to make that goal a reality.

That is what this book is about!

If you dream of recording an album, but something always seems to get in the way of you completing it; or you're a musician with the desire to perform, but you cannot see how to make it to the stage; or you have a desire to write music and share your voice and your songs with the world, this is the book for you!

I had the desire to share my voice with the world before I could even spell my name. And share it I did. I would sing and dance for anyone who would listen before I even reached kindergarten. My desire to perform and my dreams of being a singer took form when I was three years old, the moment that I first heard Elvis Presley spinning on the record player. His voice and his music unlocked some genetic coding deep within me that set me ablaze with a burning desire to sing—at THREE YEARS OLD.

I'm sure all of you have a similar experience to share. If you're reading this book, I guarantee that you've dreamed the dream of being onstage with thousands of adoring fans singing your lyrics back to you. You've dreamed of hearing your song on the radio. You've dreamed of music being more a career than a dream!

Sadly, that's where most dreamers stop. They live in the dream and rarely bother traveling the road of persistence and hard work that leads from dream to reality. It's great to dream about being on stage, writing your song, and getting your music out to the masses. But, if all you do is put your own song on repeat in your head, never bothering to get it out of your creative mind into a tangible product because you're paralyzed by the *ifs*, *whens*, *hows*, *whys*, and *whats* of releasing it, that song will never turn from dream to reality.

There are many reasons why you might not be finishing what you started. The two major roadblocks that come to mind are boredom and fear. I heard a quote today that said, "If it is important enough to you, you will find a way. If it is not, you'll find an excuse." This is a classic example of boredom. Fear is just as blameworthy. It can extinguish your dreams and desires, especially when the fear starts from within. I wonder how many great songs were never brought to light because of an artist's self-doubt.

Our goal in this book is to help YOU bring YOUR songs to life from start to finish. We aim to help you overcome your procrastinating nature, to get you out of the basement and onto the stage so that you start living and experiencing your love of music and sharing it with others. The vibration of music is a spiritual experience that can affect the emotional and physical state of not only the artist but also the listeners. If music is vibration and vibration is the foundation of our cellular existence, then it makes sense that we need music, we need more songs to carry on the vibration.

So, what is a song? Why does a song move us to intense emotional heights?

To me, a song is everything. It ties me to every memory of my life. I was telling my mom about writing this book today and she lit up with excitement. She told me that after I was born, she used to buy a new album every payday to fill the house with new music so that I would be surrounded by sound from birth. Though I was too young to remember, she told me that she played Led Zeppelin, the Beatles, Sly and the Family Stone, and Pink Floyd. She continued the tradition as I got older, branching out so that I heard Teddy Pendergrass, Bob Dylan, Willie Nelson, and so many more. So, for me, a song reflects birth and growth throughout life.

But at its core, as created by the songwriter, a song is a mental burst of creative release. It's the story of the artist, an expression of the innermost soul. It's a shared snapshot of the songwriter's life, expressed through a three-to-four-minute story relating to a personal thought, feeling, and memory, released through an audible palate of sound that has the ability to affect the emotional and physical vibration of any given listener.

A song can physically, emotionally, and spiritually affect the listener in countless ways. A song can lift you up when you are down, make your heart race with excitement, get your adrenaline pumping, your feet dancing and jumping. A song can make your heart beat faster with feelings of love. It can also make your heart ache, causing you to release tears of heartbreak over the loss of a loved one. A song can also create tears of joy. A song can even subconsciously program your mind for success.

The one universal language we all understand is "the song." We are vibratory beings by nature. Every song you write is part of your DNA. I believe we all can unlock this DNA to release the song or songs within us. There is music in every single one of us. While some of us choose to enjoy the song only by listening, others feel the calling to write, record, and release the songs within us as well as to perform these same songs for others to share in the emotional experience.

Some get stuck and never make it to the finish line, never release even one song, never take the stage to share their love of music with others. If only there were a way to eliminate those roadblocks that are preventing "stuck" musicians from reaching that finish line.

There is a way! If you have felt the calling of the songwriter, the need to release the songs within you, to hit the stage with such power that the moment you hit that drum, strum that guitar, or belt out into that microphone, you are instantly "in the zone," in that mental and physical state of utter perfection, but you have felt inhibited and unable to release the song for the world to hear, this book is for you!

Many of us can hear the songs inside us but impede the path to our own musical freedom by enacting the art of the "excuse."

I can tell you firsthand, there is no excuse valid enough to prevent you from releasing your own creativity. It is only your own personal fears stopping you from finishing that song. I understand that many of these fears may seem warranted. I've worried about not being a good enough keyboard player, not knowing how to warm up my voice. I've been scared because I had no clue how to record a song, and when I did step into a recording studio for the first time, I was very intimidated. But I reminded myself that I am a student, in fact, a lifelong student. Learning to be a better singer, to understand music theory, to learn about recording is all a part of the learning process that you can begin today by studying any music-related material. You can read an instruction book, watch a video, or hire a coach. There is NO excuse for not becoming a better student. That part, my friends, is on YOUR shoulders. Our goal here is to get you to quit procrastinating by eliminating the excuses making you lazy and fearful.

Excuses, excuses, excuses. I've met many musicians who write their own music. Some even perform a few of their own original songs live amid their set of cover band music. But, when it comes time to record and release the song, the fears and insecurities arise, leading to excuses such as, "I have writer's block" or "My songs really aren't good enough" or "I cannot afford to go into the studio."

So much time has been wasted on way too many excuses, hampering the creation of one simple, elegant creative release of beauty. Imagine if your fears ceased to exist. Imagine what beauty you could bring forth for others to hear. Imagine the amazing music you could create. Imagine the joy that YOUR song could bring to the world. Imagine how much better this world would be with more music to share.

A little warning before we move on. This book presents a path for you to follow that will help you extinguish your procrastinating nature and overcome all those excuses so that you CAN, WILL, and DO finally release those songs that exist within you. Many times our own mind gets in our way of releasing and performing our own music. But there is a way to master your mind over the control of your music. Simply put, like mind over matter, you have the ability to develop a *Mind Over Music* mentality, to induce a state of mind that will allow you to slip in and out of "the zone" for tapping into your creative nature.

If you want to live "in the zone," write and release amazing music, and perform it for all to hear, this is exactly what you'll master within these pages.

This book will not teach you the steps to writing and recording a song. It won't teach you how to play chords on a guitar or develop your singing voice. This book is not a guide to the mastery of musicianship, though I believe we never really master music; we simply continue to enjoy the creative journey, learning new steps every day. Yet the most crucial piece of the puzzle is your ability to have total *Mind Over Music* control that so many musicians lack.

In *Mind Over Music*, you'll learn how to remove all the obstacles that have been blocking your creative flow, from the first stage of writing the song to the last—finishing your creative masterpiece in the studio.

How do we accomplish this task? I hinted at it a moment ago. By finding a way to slip in and out of the zone, you will find your flow. I am sure you've heard the sayings, "I'm in the zone" and "Go with the flow" before. We aren't going to "go with the flow." We are going to become the flow. We're going to learn how to do it. When you become the flow, when you can tap into the zone, you're in rare form. Many athletes talk about being in the zone when playing basketball, football, baseball, which means to be in rare form, in peak performing condition. This is similar to achieving that runner's high during a race. There is a way to tap into the flow, to get into the zone, to find your own musical runner's high and maintain it. Simply put, it's *Mind Over Music*.

Bottom line: music is a gift. It is our responsibility to share this gift with others. Releasing the creativity within you is a selfless act, while keeping the music locked inside you, never allowing those songs to see the light of day, might be considered a selfish act.

I know at heart that we are not selfish. Creative people aren't selfish, but creative people do seem to be more intuitive to emotions, making an artist more sensitive at their core. Heightened sensitivity can lead to more fears and insecurities, which in turn lead to more excuses to avoid their creative nature. Do not fear, music is a reflection of your path through life. Your song is perfect when it comes from your inner soul. Your song is YOUR story to tell. NO fear is more powerful or more valid than your creative nature.

If you're ready to unlock your true creative potential, let's begin.

PART ONE

The Tale of Two Artists

MIND *OVER MUSIC* began as a challenge to share a method to help songwriters get from the beginning of a song idea to finishing the recording. As the method unfolded, it was evident that this process worked to help not only songwriters struggling to finish their music product but also artists who wrote music but whose fears prevented them from setting foot on stage.

To repeat, this book is not a guide to playing or learning music, and it is not a guide to overcoming stage fright. It IS a guide to overcoming fears and clearing the path for those who struggle to follow through with their ideas.

This book will help you release that story, the creativity that you've tapped into that has woken you up in the middle of the night when you hear the music coursing through your veins.

Before we begin the process, we must first understand how the idea of this book came to be. To fully understand how we can find our own flow, there are two stories to be told: my story and my mentor's story, which will lead to unlocking your full creative nature and eliminating your procrastinating nature, which will unfold in your story.

Let me first share my story.

Chapter One
THE STORY OF JAIME

SINCE I FAILED TO introduce myself in my long-winded intro, ha-ha, allow me to introduce myself now. I am Jaime Vendera, an author, singer, vocal coach, world-record holder, and above all, a dreamer.

More importantly, I am a doer of dreams. I bring to life those dreams. Even MORE importantly, I've helped others bring to life their dreams and creative thoughts. I've helped companies design new products, inspired singers to write songs, and I cannot count the times that someone I've met has said before we parted, "You make me feel like I can write a book." Many of those people DID write books.

It's true; I have an uncanny ability to tap into the creativity within myself and help others tap into their own creative mindset, and it stemmed from my own lifelong creative process.

Since I was a kid, mental movies have played out over the blank canvas of my mind, painted with all sorts of adventurous scenarios, from being a superhero to becoming a world-traveling archaeologist to interstellar space traveler to international rock star. As early as I can remember, I've always loved two things, dreaming and music.

From fifth grade on I played saxophone in school, sang in choir, performed in a theater troupe, even studied art at our local museum. I've always had the desire to engulf myself in the creative arts. I was also a songwriter. I wrote my first song in third grade while sitting in the bathtub. I was already an avid singer (in my mind), having flooded my heart, mind, and soul with every Elvis song since the age of three, dancing and singing in front of the record player at my grandmother's house for hours on end, even dancing on her coffee table for all my relatives.

You can say I had a creative spirit from an early age. So it was an easy leap for me to become a writer when my middle school English teacher presented us with a daily writing assignment in which we kept our own journals. She allowed us to write about anything we wished, whether we kept a typical diary discussing our daily thoughts and routines or tapping into our imaginations to pen fictional stories.

Writing came easy to me. I even won a writing award in high school, not that I really cared. I just loved writing, so it was no shock when at age 30 I decided it was time to write and release my first book. This would not have been possible if not for the great role models I had in school to support my passions and desires. My greatest role model was my mother.

My mom always had a positive mindset and taught me that I could achieve whatever I believed. She inspired my desire to join the local theater troupe, to sing in choir, to take art classes outside of school, to make potholders. Virtually any creative thought that came to mind, she inspired me to do it. That's why it was easy for her, even with a heavy heart, to encourage me after high school to move to Hollywood to follow my dreams of becoming a professional singer.

And follow my dreams I did. I loved singing most of all, so I decided to move to Los Angeles KNOWING that I would soon be a famous rock star.

But then the negative ticker tape took over my mind and consumed me with every single self-doubt I'd ever had about my singing and songwriting. "I wasn't a very good singer, my songs were horrible, I wasn't talented, I made a mistake by moving..."

Soooo many negative beliefs caused me to turn my back on my own self-confidence.

Within a year, I came home from L.A. with my tail between my legs. Yet that desire to play music still burned within me, albeit only a few small embers at that point. I'd lost the true passion I had for music that had burned bright within me just a few years before. I'd lost my days of being consumed by music, when songs would play on MTV and I'd run out and buy an artist's record and play it over and over and over again until I knew every word and nuance of the song by heart, until I could play the entire record in my mind without even hearing the actual song.

Though something had changed within me, it didn't mean my love of music was gone. I missed music, and I knew I'd lost my musical fire. I felt like it was the end of a relationship, like my true love had left me. But I knew there must be some way to rekindle our love affair.

Eventually, I began to fight to bring back my true love of music. It was a struggle. I weaved in and out of bands for many years before I took a good hard look at why I was blocked and inhibited.

I finally figured it out. My fire had dimmed because I was being choked by the fumes of my own self-defeating thoughts, which were extinguishing my passion to sing, write, perform, and record. I was gasping on fumes, losing the battle, until I realized that it was ME creating the resistance. Once I realized that I controlled my creative outcome, I knew that all I had to do was set my own goal, stomp out those negative thoughts, and take action!!!!

Take action I did, but not in the way I expected. I "accidentally"" became a vocal coach in 1996 when a friend wanted to know my "secret" for singing high notes. I didn't really have an answer. But as he asked me about it, my first semiofficial voice lesson took place. I created a new vocal exercise on the spot and within 45 minutes I had created the bones of my own vocal method, which helped my friend Troy sing higher and freer than he ever had in his life.

A light went off in my head. I had not only created the framework for a new vocal method but also stumbled upon a "method" for overcoming my own fears. Since that time, I've used this simple method to overcome many obstacles in my life. This method is simple:

1. Set a specific goal!
2. Eliminate fears and excuses!
3. Take action!

This method has helped me set a world glass-shattering record, travel the world appearing on countless television shows and conducting workshops, write dozens of books, create other products, become a vocal coach—even training some of my own musical idols—and start my own online school. I found my self-confidence again by tapping into the creative force that had been a part of me since childhood.

So you see, the creative force runs strong with this one, hahaha, but it runs strong with all of you, too!

Still, my creative force wasn't leading me to fulfill my true passion, which is writing more songs. I'd become a success in my own right in other fields. The writing, TV, and coaching had filled some of the void in my life, but a piece of my heart—the music—stayed empty. Though the music kept playing in my mind, I had come to accept that my creative path was that of a book writer, glass shatterer, and vocal coach. I needed to leave the job of "songwriter" to my students.

But deep in my heart, I couldn't accept it. When I realized I was still avoiding the true love in my life, I began a new journey to find out what was still blocking me in the one area that was missing in my life. I prayed and begged for guidance, and then something happened. One of my favorite authors, Joe Vitale (*Attractor Factor, At Zero*, etc.), had announced that he was putting out his own record. I hadn't paid it much attention until a few years later when I realized that Joe's "one album" had turned into two, into three, into fifteen albums he'd released within only a few years.

I was amazed, blown away actually, and inspired enough to start writing my own songs again. I soon released two songs. I wanted to release more, but I was overwhelmed with everything else in my life. And songs just weren't flowing out of me. While I was inspired by Joe's capacity for songwriting, I fell back into my "acceptance of failure" as if it were the norm.

Then one day, an order came in to my website. Someone named "Joe Vitale" had ordered my books. Curious, I reached out to him to see if it was THE Joe Vitale of movies like *The Secret*. To my surprise, it was.

I had always wondered, "What makes Joe tick? How did this non-musician release so many albums in so few years?"

Now I had the chance to ask the man himself. So I asked. Okay, I begged and pleaded for an interview with him, and he obliged. The interview was truly an eye-opener, and by picking Joe's mind, I found my musical roots once again. Which leads me to his story.

Chapter Two
THE STORY OF JOE

IT IS ALMOST IRONIC HOW THE SYNCHRONICITIES of our lives are intertwined at every turn, though most fail to recognize these connections. I've failed multiple times, until I learned to look for and appreciate all the connections that lie between each of us.

As I was driving to my vocal studio in Columbus, Ohio, one day (I live two hours away), I was in awe, thinking of how the tiny little winding backroad I was navigating connected me straight to the fast-paced city street 100 miles away where I taught voice. Though I always lived by the understanding that we are all connected, this moment made it real for me. Which is why I knew that Joe Vitale's story was already connected to mine, which led me to this interview.

Once Joe agreed to the interview, I wrote down every question that popped into my head, knowing he had made the connections to THE answer for overcoming the mental obstacles blocking me and so many others like myself from becoming a start-to-finish songwriter. I wanted to know where his love of music came from, how he got started, how he wrote so many songs so fast, where he got all his musical talent, what was his musical background. I had my own answers to these questions, but I wanted to know if his answers had helped him pave a different path to success.

To my surprise, he said he had next to no musical background. He wanted to play guitar at ten, but his dad bought him an accordion instead and signed him up for accordion lessons, which lasted until he got bored.

Still, he had a secret desire to be a musician that he carried throughout his life. He'd buy guitars for himself occasionally, as rewards, but never really played them, even admitting that he only knew three chords. He even picked up a harmonica about 25 years ago. His musical background consisted of little to no lessons, no real musical upbringing besides the radio, but a burning desire to become a musician. That desire inside him was never extinguished.

Yet for decades, his path did not lead him to the calling of musician. So how did this man with virtually no musical background become a professional musician in his late 50s?

The answer is quite simple. At end of 2010, at 57 years old, Joe asked himself a question:

"What is left undone?"

He wanted to become an author, he wanted to be in movies, he wanted to go around the world, and he'd done them all. Close to a hundred books, dozens of movies, countless trips to the far reaches of the globe, all accomplished.

Still, he wondered, *"What is left undone?"*

In that moment he realized that the music was what was left undone. He wanted to write his own songs, sing and play them, and record them. It was on his bucket list. It had been for almost half a century. Now it was time to check it off his list.

In that moment, he decided he was going to become the musician that lingered inside him. He felt the passion stir stronger, and even without knowing the *hows*, *whens*, or *whys*, he set his mind on his goal.

But the first thing that happened to Joe when he decided to write his own songs was that all his self-doubts came to the surface. It scared him.

Sound familiar? I know it rings a bell with me.

Everything about "I cannot do that" came to the forefront of his mind.

I couldn't believe it. Here was this man I considered to be one of the most positive role models in my life and thousands of other lives admitting to me that he'd had self-doubt.

Then the truth hit me. We are all human, and unfortunately, as humans, we have a tendency to doubt our decisions and dreams. Joe had doubts just like any other human. I had self-doubt, too. WE ALL have self-doubt. It affects us all.

However, he did what many fail to do. He CHOSE not to allow his doubt to forge his path. He faced every doubt that surfaced. He cleared every one of them! He eradicated them from his mind, erasing all the limiting beliefs in his head to get free of his own negative beliefs.

As the negative beliefs, one by one, dissolved into nothing, he set the intention to write and record his own album and went to work toward his goal. He didn't wait around for it to manifest. He put his intention into action by filling his mind with all things music, by using his body to practice developing all the skills required to play music. He got a vocal coach, he hired a guitar teacher, he even went into a recording studio to learn about the process.

He also did something that was crucial to his success: He gave himself one year to do his first album, deciding that it would be the perfect Christmas present at the end of 2011.

Ironically, at the same time, a magazine contacted him for an interview and asked him about being on the cover of a future issue. He asked what they wanted to discuss, and they said the story could be about whatever he wished. He knew that the magazine would be the perfect opportunity to present himself to the world as a singer-songwriter.

But when they said they wanted him on the cover in three months, he decided his 12-month plan was now shortened by three quarters. Undeterred, he changed his intention and contacted everyone who would be involved in the recording process.

Synchronicity? A push from the universe to put into action the steps required to make his intention a reality??? I believe so!

Did he make his deadline? Indeed, he did!

Joe Vitale wrote and recorded his first album, *Blue Healer*, in only three months. He met his new deadline and was featured on the cover of the magazine with his first album.

My interview with Joe was in 2015. At the time of the interview he had already released over a dozen albums, including five singer-songwriter albums, with not one, but two albums released in 2011. As I write this (January 2018) Joe has now released 15 albums! He's won many awards for his music and even released an album of sax music.

Sax? You heard me correctly.

He decided he wanted to play sax. He knew nothing could stop his intentions. He'd heard a baritone saxophone and loved it, so he decided it was time to learn a new instrument.

He had a sax player come into the studio to record some parts for one of his albums and started asking him questions. He ordered a vintage baritone sax, and when it arrived he had no clue even how to put it together. So he hired a sax teacher for one hour, and the teacher showed him how to put the sax together and play his first sounds. The teacher told him he had a natural talent. Joe laughed and wondered if it were true or the teacher was just stroking his ego.

He set his intention to learn how to play the sax, and he was putting it into action! After that initial lesson, he went home and watched three videos on how to play saxophone and kept practicing what he'd learned.

He learned that jazz saxophonist Mindi Abair was marketing a fundraising campaign for one of her CDs. One of the perks she was offering was a sax lesson. He bought one, did the Skype lesson with her, and asked her a laundry list of questions. (Same as I did to Joe during our interview, ha-ha.) She happily answered every one.

Armed with woodwind knowledge, he decided to make a full-blown sax record. All his sax learning and recording happened within six months, leading to him write and record his own album of baritone swagger.

Joe had followed his heart, his gut instinct, his intuition, which had been guiding him his entire life toward his burning desire to become a musician. Once he set his intentions, he followed through on every musical intention he declared. From his burning desire he created a bluesy, rock, somewhat folky style of music, singing and playing guitar on all his albums, even playing sax, all without having ANY true musical background until his intention to start working on his musical bucket list in 2010.

Even now, he says that music is an ongoing creative learning experience, and he is still finding his way every single day, expressing what makes him joyful. It shows in his music. He wanted his music to be self-help-oriented to make people happy and boost them, much like his books, audio programs, videos, and movies. His songwriting was musically and lyrically layered with words and textures designed for programming you for success.

Because this man faced his own doubts, cleared them, and intended to become a musician, he found his own musical path and style.

Still, there had to be an underlying theme that allowed him to beat down the wall of procrastination and break the chains of self-doubt. I had to master this theme, this "secret" for music success. So I asked him to share with me his secret for becoming a professional musician in such a short time.

There must be a secret that separates the doers from the dreamers. Being a vocal coach, I had seen many singers and musicians who dreamed about writing and releasing their own music, but many were falling short, never doing anything to follow through on their dreams. (I've also taught many doers, who instinctively follow the same steps in this book.)

Many musicians stagnated before finishing the process, worried about the ins and outs of writing and recording, worried about how to pay for recording, scared that writer's block would impede their creative journey, doubting their own abilities. They had many of the same self-doubts that Joe had experienced.

In fact, as I write this, I noticed a post on social media from a guitarist complaining that every time he records an album, he can never find a singer to record the vocals. In my mind, I see an opportunity for this guitarist to expand his musical horizons to develop his own voice. I kept silent but read the responses. They were heartbreaking. Many singers responded that they wanted to do it, but made excuses like, "I would if only I had a recording studio" and "If you can wait one year, while I train really hard, I think I could sing for you."

There is too much self-doubt that prevents artistic creation, and it spreads like an infection when those doubts are reinforced by such excuse-ridden comments.

Excuses are a disease, and it's time for the cure! I believed that Joe had the cure. So again, I asked him what his secret was for musical success, and he replied, "THE SECRET for becoming successful in every field, whether it is music or business or becoming an author, is that the individual has GOT to get CLEAR of the negative limiting excuses in their head."

I wondered if anyone could do this or was Joe some special positivity alien sent from Mars, ha-ha.

But that is not the case; he is human like the rest of us. He humbly says that he is not special, that he has no hidden talent, only his positive mindset, fueled by his ability to clear out his negative chatter and put his intentions into action!

He acknowledged that you must look at what you're thinking because you either block or release your own creativity and success. If you're having doubt and making excuses and not getting anything done, it is your own negative beliefs that are inhibiting you.

And again, we ALL have self-sabotaging, negative thoughts at times. But YOUR success depends on what YOU decide to do with those thoughts. Do you claim them or clear them?

When Joe's inhibitive thoughts arose, he clearly stated his intention to write and record his first album, and then he cleared every negative belief that was inhibiting his true intention.

He even recalled an inspiring quote that helped him through the process:

"WHERE IS THE PROOF???"

Four simple words he'd heard from songwriters Ray Wiley Hubbard and Kevin Welch during a songwriting workshop.

They challenged him in many ways and made him question, in a positive manner, every step he needed to take to release his album:

"Where is the proof that you cannot put the album out?"

"Where is the proof that you cannot sing?"

"Where is the proof that you can't play guitar?"

"Where is the proof that you can't be a star?"

THERE ISN'T ANY PROOF!!!

If you think you have proof that you cannot do any of these things, PLEASE try to show us. I dare you.

THERE ISN'T ANY PROOF!

Joe even questioned my thinking. In the interview he said,

"There is an old saying that goes, *it is what it is*, which is a simple defeat or acceptance of a circumstantial situation that you have no control over. To become that songwriter you wish to be, you got to get past *it is what it is*, because there is no proof that it is what it is."

I am guilty of using this saying hundreds if not thousands of times. Joe has a better saying, and he wears it proudly on a purple T-shirt it to prove it. That saying is,

"IT IS WHAT YOU ACCEPT"

He spreads the slogan everywhere and lives by it.

Case in point: Joe recorded one of his albums, *Strut*, in only two days. During the long process, he could feel his throat tightening, becoming worn from all the recording. He could have thought, "It is what it is," but he knew in truth that "It is what you accept." He did not accept his situation, so he used all the tips and tricks he'd learned about singing (some from my books) to keep his voice in shape. :)

More importantly, it wasn't about my vocal books. It was about

Joe taking action!!! He refused to fall into the negative mindset. Instead, he chose to act!

He'd applied this formula throughout his life, even used it to release four albums in record time. However, after Joe's fourth album, he felt musically dry and dead inside and thought he was done. Yet he knew there was an ever-existing, creative stream in our lives. He thought that maybe he could tap into it for another album; or maybe he was done.

Faced with this choice, Joe made a declaration that he was going into the studio in two months to record ten new original songs. Though he felt as if he was dried up, he still made the intention.

The strangest (actually, the most obvious) thing happened that night. A song came to him. The next day, two more songs flooded his mind. Within a few weeks he had 30 songs from nothing. His mindset went from having no songs to having 30 songs from which he could pick the ten for his next album. That album was *Sun Will Rise*.

Hopefully you're beginning to see the common thread between our two stories. Let me sum up Joe's formula for his musical success:

1. KNOW and STATE your intention. Know what you want (instead of thinking, "How can I write, what will I write, how will I record?"). Once you know what you want, set a goal and set a deadline. Once the deadline is set, everything starts falling into place.
2. Start clearing your negative beliefs as they surface in your mind.
3. Start taking action toward reaching your deadline.

I was shocked that these three steps were so simple. They were the same three steps I had used starting all those years ago, which led to me releasing my first book, achieving my desire to be on television, and so much more. I realized it truly was that simple:

1. Set a specific goal/State your intention
2. Eliminate your fears and excuses/Clear your negative thoughts
3. Take action/Start taking action

WOW, our three steps were identical, save for the wording. All along I had the ability to release ANY part of my creative life, but I'd never applied it to music. Since opening up my mindset, new songs and music-related programs have flowed to me. I had negative beliefs, such as "I can't do this on my own," "I need a songwriting partner," "I need a better mic," "I need an engineer..." At the core, none of these were true. There was no proof that I could not make my love of music a reality.

To sum up the story of us and help you apply it to your own musical life, know that there is no proof that you cannot accomplish your music. You just need the burning desire, and then you need to state it as an intention, clear your own negative beliefs, and put it into action.

I've listened to Joe's interview many times because it is so inspiring. In fact, I told Joe that he should write a book about releasing the musician within. I originally wanted him to write a book about getting into the zone. I even had a really cool name for it, *Own the Zone*. But, alas, it wasn't in the cards. It just didn't feel like it was time.

As time went by, one morning I woke up with this burning voice telling me that it was finally time for that book to be written. But my sense of the main focus of the book had shifted. I messaged Joe and said something like,

"Listen up, Vitale, the Universe smacked me again to put this in your brain...and I am pretty sure I told you this a few years back:) You REALLY need to write an "LOA/Ramp up your music making mojo" type book. It's not a book about the art of songwriting, but more a book lining out the steps to get a musician off their butt and finishing their songs and recording/releasing them...You are THE perfect person to write this considering what you've accomplished!!! If you don't write this, that voice in my head will never leave me alone. It will pester me to pester you until you hear it too;) There, I told you, just as I was instructed to do. So now please write the book so it will make the voices stop, hahahaha;)"

His reply?

"Hmmmm, maybe it's in your head and not mine. So you write it and I add to it to be coauthor..."

So there you have it. We did it. Our two stories have given you all the steps to unleash the musician within. That's it, the book is done, three simple steps.

Just teasing. There is more to the story. Now it is time to help you put all three steps into order so that YOU become the musician you've always desired to be.

PART TWO

The Story of You

YOUR STORY IS WHERE your real musical adventure begins! Are you ready to unlock your true creative potential, quit procrastinating, and get your music out to the masses?
YES, YOU ARE!!!
Why I even bothered to ask you is beyond me. :)
To begin this process, you must tell the story of you. Better yet, it is time to RELIVE the story of YOU.
There is a lot to cover before we begin applying the three steps to musical freedom. The first step is to review your life. Search your memories to find the initial spark that drew you into music. Recall those times when you were consumed by music, those days and nights when you blared the radio or played your mp3s, CDs, cassettes, even 8-tracks over and over and over again. Then recall when YOU stepped into the world of playing music, becoming the pilot of the song by stepping into the role of the artist, learning to play other artist's songs, as well as creating your own.
By remembering and reliving the passionate, music-related scenarios of your past, YOUR key moments when you were totally consumed by music, you'll begin to understand that you instinctively set goals, stated intentions, eliminated your excuses, cleared your negative beliefs, and took action every time you were consumed by music.
These were the times you were in a state of perfect flow, you were in the zone, and so in sync with the music, so in love and lost in the music that every song embedded a key uplifting memory in your mind.
This process is simple and it works! Let's begin by discovering the origin of your musical fire.

Chapter Three
DISCOVERING THE ORIGIN OF YOUR MUSICAL FIRE

ARE YOU READY TO ROCK! Notice I didn't "ask" if you were ready to rock, because I know you are. So grab a notebook, because you'll be writing down a LOT of your past memories. If you prefer, you can skip the pen and paper and keep track of those memories on your smartphone, tablet, Mac, or PC in a digital notepad or Word document. Regardless, you do need a way to keep track before we begin this process.

If you're writing in a notebook or diary, on the very first page or on the cover, please write:

MIND OVER MUSIC WORKBOOK

Label your Word document, Notepad document, Google document, or whatever digital format you're using with the same name.

Now that you're ready to begin, think back over your life and answer the following questions:

1. *When was the very first time you were pulled into music?* In other words, what is your earliest memory of the very first song that sucked you into the music? What was it about that song or album that pulled you in? Was it the singer's voice? The

tone of the guitar? The style of music?

2. *What songs did you play over and over and over again?* Go ahead, make a big list. I want to know EVERY song and album that resonated through every cell of your soul! In addition, you need to thoroughly dissect each song and each album to find out what made you so insanely nuts about the music. There is a reason that certain songs and albums speak to you. It could be the singer, the guitar player, the piano parts, the beat of the drum and rhythm of the bass, or the subject of the lyrical content. All this information is extremely important.

3. *Recall those times when you were in the zone and accomplished/finished something music-related.* In other words, this question steps beyond being a "listener" of music into becoming the musician. I want you to remember those moments in your life when you were playing music, whether at practice, at a gig, or recording in a studio when you felt so in tune with the music that every note floated out of you.

4. *When (if at all) did you notice a change in how you felt about music in general?* (When did the fire start to dim?) Can you recall a key moment in your past when listening to music lost that all-consuming spark you once had? When did you stop playing any albums and/or specific songs over and over again? When did you lose interest in rehearsing with a band, performing, writing music, or recording music?

These questions will serve as sections in your *Mind Over Music* workbook. It is easy to create sections in a digital format, but if you're writing by hand in a diary or notebook, please leave at least 10 pages between each question, writing the question down (in order) at the top of a page. Now, let's pause and reflect on your past to answer these questions.

Take your time and be thorough. Add as many details to describe every memory, whether it is the memory of a girlfriend or boyfriend, or a memory of heartbreak or excitement. All thoughts that pertain to any given memory are markers explaining why each song and album pulled you into the music. In case you need some guidance, here are a few of my answers:

When was the very first time you were pulled into music?

I was three years old and I heard "Jailhouse Rock" by Elvis Presley spinning on my grandmother's record player. I was running through her kitchen into the adjoining room that led down a hallway. I was at full speed and in my socks. But as I rounded the corner from the kitchen and heard that angelic voice, it stopped me in my tracks. Well, I slid a few feet until I came to a halt, ha-ha. Regardless, I quit running and got lost in the sound of Elvis's voice. There was something about that slight aggression in his voice that pulled me in. The way the guitars started with staccato chord strums grabbed me too. I sat down and listened to the entire record, including songs like "Hound Dog" and "Teddy Bear." I loved how his voice took on a deeper tone on songs like "Teddy Bear." I was hooked.

What songs did you play over and over and over again?

As an 80s kid, I played both pop and rock records over and over again, including *Pyromania* by Def Leppard, *Ready for the World* (self-titled), *Around the World in a Day* by Prince, *BulletBoys* (self-titled), *Let's Go All the Way* by Sly Fox, *All That Jazz* by Breathe, and *All Systems Go* by Vinnie Vincent Invasion. I was consumed by these soundtracks. Being a singer, I always focus on the vocals. Each of these singers had something in their voice that pulled me. I could love totally different singers for different reasons. For example, with Joe Elliott (Def Leppard), it was his range and rasp, while Melvin Riley (Ready for the World) had this super soulful seductive cry when he sang, without even needing a lot of vocal range.

I remember listening to the song "Hands to Heaven" by Breathe over and over again on the cassette single so many times that I burned up the cassette and had to buy another copy. Every time I listened to it I thought my heart would explode. I was with my first true love, and my job right out of high school allowed me to listen to music all day. That song was my anchor to her, knowing I'd see her after work.

BulletBoys, on the other hand, got me wired. It was like "music caffeine" for my mind and body. I was cranked up and ready to roll when I listened to their music. In fact, as I write this, I realize that the first three BulletBoys records were always on PLAY in my jambox, back when cassettes were the norm. I still listen to them, although I've upgraded from cassettes to CDs and finally playlists on my iPhone. Sadly, I didn't care for the third BulletBoys record, but I was an avid fan, so I still consumed the third record. As I am writing, I decided to play *Za-Za,* and though I didn't care for it nearly as much as their first two releases, I still remember every song and all the lyrics. Ironically, BulletBoys have since released five other albums full of original music, and I've bought every release. But I've never played them over and over again, so none of the later songs pull me in, though they are still one of my favorite bands.

Recall those times when you were in the zone and accomplished/ finished something music-related.

I have to mention several. I recall my first Christmas play, when I was in 5th grade. I was consumed with learning the two songs I had to sing and remembering every line I had to speak. I was in the zone when I performed that play. The songs floated out of me and I knew every line as if they were my own words. Performing so well in that play helped me land a spot in a theater troupe at our local museum.

I also recall playing in a club in 1991 with my original band, Chained Angel. It was the end of our set, and one of the guitarists, David Noble, went right into an original song called "Sweating Bullets," which was supposed to be the first song of our next set. But something drew him into the song and the rest of the band followed along. I jumped right into singing, and the rest of the band, Scott Stith, Lonnie Winters, and Jeff Wright, fell right into the jam like a well-oiled machine. As we finished the song and I walked off stage, I was stopped by a fellow musician who said,

"Jaime, that song was amazing! 'Sweating Bullets' is a hit!"

I smiled, but I was kind of confused, because this was the first night we were to ever play "Sweating Bullets" live, and we weren't playing it until next set. I said, "Thanks, yeah, we will play Sweating Bullets next set." He looked at me funny while I walked away. It took me a few minutes to even realize that we had just played the song. I was so in the zone, so in sync and in love with the music, so well-rehearsed for our show from countless band practices that I HAD NO CLUE we had just played "Sweating Bullets." It was as if I was on autopilot. That memory is a great example of a passionate musical moment where I was so on fire and passionate about playing music that I felt like I had been elevated to another plane of existence. I was in the zone, but it felt like I was inside a dream.

If I am to be honest, I have only been completely 100% "in the zone," where I felt like I was inside a dream, but a handful of times in my life. But I have a feeling that this book holds the key for ALL OF US to exist in the zone for every performance and recording session so that we do see the music through until the final step of the process, where the show is revealed to an audience and the song is unveiled to the world.

Since I am on a roll, let me tell you of the one other time where I was so in the zone that I felt like I was dreaming. I had been asked to appear on the show *Good Morning America* to perform an amazing feat—shattering a glass with my voice. I had been asked by my vocal coach, Jim Gillette, to appear in his place when he was asked to perform this feat for the hosts of Discovery Channel's *MythBusters*. Since he was too busy to make the flight he called me up and asked me, as his protege, to shatter a glass with an amplifier. I was instantly in fear. He assured me that he could teach me, but that didn't prevent doubt from flooding my mind. Still, I could not let my coach, my singing idol, down, so I said, "YES, I will do this, and I can do this."

I had only had a few weeks to prepare, so I became consumed with learning how to shatter glass. Though Jim had walked me through step by step, at first it was very rough. But I was diligent and set my mind on accomplishing my goal, and within a few hours I had shattered my first glass with the aid of an amplifier. The show was several weeks later. I arrived In New York late on Saturday night, and much to my surprise, the very next morning I was met with over twenty other opera singers who were called in for me to train as my opponent for the live Monday morning show. I had no idea this was going to happen. I could have balked and refused and been angry, but the vocal coach in me took it as an opportunity to work with more students. So I gave it my all in training them and had a wonderful day. Even after eight hours of screaming, my voice felt amazing.

The next morning, which was the day of the show, I was so nervous. To calm my nerves, I visualized the show in my mind as if it had already occurred. Eventually, it flashed before my eyes like a show on a TV screen. It was so real, it startled me. So I let it flow and allowed myself to drift into the zone. I lived it out in my mind, and the moment I was on camera, I was completely in the zone. To date, it was my most flawless, effortless glass-shattering show. That one show set the path for me to perform on dozens of shows around the world. It set me on fire and I kept the fire burning. This first show reignited my passion for voice and drove me to work harder at training other singers.

While this isn't really a "song" or "band" example, it is an example of how practice doesn't just make perfect, but practice makes opportunities to get your mind and body into the zone. Plus, you can see how it pulled me back into music.

Now it's your turn to share. Open up that *Mind Over Music* workbook and write down all your memories in great detail for the following questions.

When was the very first time you were pulled into music?

What was YOUR first musical moment? Was it in when you heard a certain song on the radio when you were 15? What drew you into the song? Was it the sound of the guitar, the beat of the drum, the tone of the singer's voice that connected you to the song? Did the music light an emotional fire so strong within you that you could listen to a song or an entire album over and over and over again?

What songs did you play over and over and over again?

PLEASE take your time with this question. I want you to remember EVERY song and album that you played on repeat. These are the songs of your musical birth that lit the fire within you. Even if you don't listen to those musical styles anymore, they are still the catalysts that started the fire.

Recall those times when you were in the zone and accomplished/finished something music-related.

Do you remember a time when you were in a recording studio and the session went so amazing that you were blown away by the finished product? Or how about a time you were on stage and the audience was going insane watching and listening to you perform? When was the last time that YOU remember having a defining musical moment? A time when you were so consumed by writing, recording, or performing that you felt like you were experiencing runner's high, felt as if you were in the zone, and the music flowed out of you like water. What musical performance/recording moments can you recall when you were on fire?

I repeat, look back in your life and write down every single memory relating to each question in great detail. This is an important rite of passage in preparing you to overcome any boundaries that you've created to prevent you from achieving musical success.

Why is this so important?

Because one of the biggest reasons a musician doesn't follow through from start to finish is a "loss of fire." (But you'll soon learn that recalling these magical moments can help to rekindle that fire.)

Sometimes, as our lives progress, though we didn't wish it to happen, we still created a situation or situations that led to losing the fire for music. We might not have even realized it as it was happening. When we lose that strong emotional connection, those flames of passion and creativity might begin to dim, not burning as brightly in your life right now as they did years ago.

Or maybe they are still burning bright, and you still believe you feel as passionate about music today as the first day you discovered music, but you're not finishing your songs or performing regularly. If so, then something in your life is impeding the process, whether it was caused by boredom or fear (which we will cover soon).

So, stop reading right now and review your final answer to this question, if you've already written down all your memories. If not, it is time to write down all those defining moments when you were consumed by music and felt as if you were in the zone. Your memories are personal and all about YOUR musical journey, and they can help you figure out what it takes to keep the fire going.

Let's review your memory list. Did you recall a time when you were asked to join a band and had to learn 60 songs by the coming weekend, so you lived and breathed those songs, did the gig, and amazed yourself?

Maybe there was a time in your young life when you wanted the lead role in a high school play. You were only a sophomore, and generally the lead went to a senior. Nevertheless, you set it in your mind that you could be and would be the lead role, despite being a sophomore. You studied every line until you knew the entire play by heart, you practiced the songs until you could sing them in your sleep. Come the day of auditions, you gave it everything you had and landed that lead role.

Or maybe you were a solo artist and there was a time when you went into a local recording studio on a whim to record a love song that you'd written for your boyfriend or girlfriend. The recording session flowed, and you knocked every part out in a few takes.

Bottom line, dig deep and grab every memory you can. These are gifts of music, the reason we love music. Cherish them as you remember them. Let's move on so you can understand how these memories can make your passion for music burn so hot that you'll be cranking out tunes like clockwork and become a performing/recording machine.

This is really important. I hope you're writing down every single memory!!!

Now let's go deeper and remember the sensation of feeling the fire.

Chapter Four
FEELING THE FIRE

IF FOR SOME REASON you aren't finishing your songs, all you need is to be reminded of the fire that turned you into a songwriter in the first place. To remember what the fire feels like, you need to discover what ignites that fire, what sparks your creativity and passion.

Psssst—you've already been working on recalling what sparks your creativity and passion!

That's the reason I had you recall all those incredibly fond memories of your past major musical moments. I wanted you to feel that raging fire again, if only for a moment. I wanted you to remember how it felt, how hungry you were for the music, by remembering all those times when you were so consumed by the music that you got lost in every chord, every beat of the drum, every lyric that you heard or that you sang. I wanted you to remember what it felt like to be in the zone.

Within those memories exist certain triggers that sparked your passion for music. Now that we have a list of our positive musical memories, we have a list within each of those memories of certain "triggers" that put you in a positive mindset that inspired you to listen to music, to write music, to play music.

Time for more reflection. Please review every entry in your pages of memories. BUT, as you sift through each memory, you must look for similarities between the memories. You need to find the common threads that connect all those musical memories together. Once you find a similarity, you can write it down in a new section in your notebook or on your notepad. This will be the first step in creating a personal list that I call your "motivational sparks of creativity" list.

I know this is a big assignment, and it might feel time consuming, but it is VERY important to your musical success. So stop here and review each of your memories to find those common thread triggers that ignited your love for music and sparked the fire of your creativity.

Here are a few entries from my motivational sparks of creativity list:

- ✓ When other people heard me sing and smiled.
- ✓ When the audience applauded.
- ✓ When I saw someone singing along to the song as I sang.
- ✓ Whenever I am singing songs with lots of energy. This is generally rock music or upbeat pop music for me.
- ✓ Writing songs that have lots of meaningful lyrics related to memories in my life.
- ✓ When my songwriting partner and I write a song that comes together so quickly it was as if we were writing from one shared mind.
- ✓ When my band locks in during rehearsal and the songs flow.
- ✓ When the recording engineer gives me the thumbs up.

When I knew I would be performing in front of a large audience, I got fired up. If I knew I was singing hard-driven rock songs with high notes and lots of energy, I was fired up. If I was writing an original song with lyrics that had meaning to my life, I was fired up. When someone smiled, sang along, or gave me the thumbs up, I was fired up.

Whenever I was "sparked" or knew I would be in a situation that would spark me, I worked hard to achieve my goal, to prepare for the gig, to finishing writing the song.

Now make YOUR list of motivational sparks of creativity. Once you've finished your list, review each "spark." In the future, once we start living by the three steps, you will do everything possible to make sure you are putting those motivational sparks of creativity into every musical situation you have, to assure success. Don't worry about "how" you'll do this, because we will cover that later. For now, just make that list!

You probably think from my list that ALL my musical encounters were amazing. Not so. I wasn't always sparked during every rehearsal, gig, or recording session. Take songwriting, for example. I have written lots of duds or written with partners where I just didn't feel the same enthusiasm they did for a particular song. If I was writing a song that didn't spark my creativity, that didn't interest me, minutes turned to hours as I worked on the song. Boredom would set in. I would lose my lyrical focus and blame the stagnation on "writer's block."

But when I was fired up, boy did I work for it!!! And those hours spent writing a song flew by like seconds.

I have this shirt that says, "Winners Train, Losers Complain." I used to wear it in videos for my school, Vendera Vocal Academy, to instill a positive "practice" mindset into my singers' minds. While I am not trying to harsh your mellow and saying, "Hey you, quit being a complainer," I AM trying to point out that every one of us can bear this faulty trait at times. We either want something, or we don't. It is that simple.

Remember, "If it is important enough to you, you will find a way. If it is not, you'll find an excuse." During those times when the spark isn't so intense, you might feel bored with music. For example, you joined a new band and the first three weeks you had a blast. But you're already growing bored at rehearsal and starting to think of ways to leave early or skip practice altogether. And you don't get it. You couldn't wait to join this band, and now you don't understand WHY you're feeling this way.

Boredom can exist to help remind you of what you do and do not want out of music. In these moments of boredom, you might think you want something, such as to play with that band, but in truth, you might possibly not. Maybe the band doesn't inspire your creative spark. Or maybe music isn't as important to you as you thought.

Still, we might REALLY want it bad and truly want to rehearse with this particular band to create something memorable, but you are having trouble remembering the chords and lyrics to a song, or you are having mental blocks writing a song with the band. Yet you KNOW you love playing and writing as much as the very first day you became a musician. But issues still arise to block your flow.

In these instances, it could be your own fear blocking you. So let's move beyond those motivational sparks of creativity and discuss what could possibly create a block in our flow. Let's learn what causes our fire to dim and discover what we can do to rekindle that fire.

Chapter Five
WHEN THE FIRE DIMS

I BET YOU'VE BEEN WONDERING, "What happened to question #4?" I've been saving it for a chapter of its own, hahaha.

When (if at all) did you notice a change in how you felt about music in general? (When did the fire start to dim?)
This one's a doozy. Some of us have lost our flame or have noticed that our spark of creativity has begun to dull. Most of the musicians I've worked with have told me that their fiery passion and love for music has dimmed slightly over the years. I will assume it's the same for you, or else you wouldn't be reading this book trying to figure out how to quit procrastinating and finish what you started.

If you're guilty of procrastination, have failed to put together that amazing band or finished recording your album, then you've lost some of the fire. A loss of fire signals that you're experiencing boredom or fear. Not to worry; if your fire has dulled, even slightly, all you need to do is reignite that fire to get back on the path.

Now that we've discovered our motivational sparks of creativity—i.e., what sparks our creativity and musical drive—all that's left is to discover what has put out that fire. There are two reasons you are losing the fire, which could prevent you from becoming a better musician, hamper your ability to write more songs, inhibit you from "getting fired up."

You've guessed it; the two major fire extinguishers in a musician's life are:

1. **Boredom**—If you do not have the fire, if that fire has dulled, boredom could be the culprit.
2. **Fear**—Fear of your own musical ability and talent is equally guilty.

Let's review each in detail:

Boredom

Boredom is a sure sign of lack of interest or lack of passion. I am not saying this is always a negative thing. I hate sports. It's just not me. When my cousins wanted to play softball or shoot hoops, I was bored out of my mind. I just didn't have any passion for it.

I've also been bored many times with music. I couldn't learn certain songs, because I didn't like them, and I never recorded the originals I wrote years ago, because they didn't excite me. Looking back, I now realize that I wasn't as interested in the songs I wrote years ago as I thought I was. Sound familiar?

Many people love dreaming the dream but do not love "achieving" the dream. I think when I was in my twenties, I was more in love with the dreaming than the doing. I can recall being in some bands that didn't excite me, writing music or learning covers just for the sake of being part of something. My boredom for that style of music far outweighed my love for music in general, which is why I experienced writer's block, or wrote subpar songs with stupid lyrics just to say that I finished writing a tune.

I personally am NOT a fan of hearing the words "Writer's Block." I believe you are either on fire to write or you're just bored and uninspired. After you finish this book, you'll feel the same way. However, I have experienced those moments of being creatively dead and feeling like I'd never write a song again. Now that I have a great songwriting partner and also write the music I want to write, I never feel this way.

It is now time to seek out where the boredom started to appear in your musical timeline. We will break this into two parts: listening to music and writing/performing music. Let's start with the act of listening to music. Ask yourself,

When (if at all) did I notice a change in how I felt about music? When did the fire start to dim?

When was the very last time you had that feeling to listen to a song or record over and over and over again? This would be the last entry on your list of songs/records for Question #2. It could have been twenty years ago, last summer, last week, or maybe you are still consumed by music the same way you were as a teenager. Therefore, your last answer is what you are consumed by today. Congratulations, I am soooo happy that you still have that fire for listening to music going full blast!

For those of you who have felt the fire dim a bit, not to worry, we will get it back!

If I am going to be honest, as I started writing this book I really had no idea how I was going to line out the program. But, as it unfolded in my mind, it made me face some tough questions. It made me realize that the last time I was totally on fire for music was way back in 1995 when I was consumed by the album *Wait* by Steelheart. I listened to that album over and over and over again, just like all those albums from my teen years.

I have enjoyed lots of records since 1995, but that was the last time I recall being completely consumed with playing an entire album over and over again.

As far as one single song that I played on repeat, it was a little closer in my timeline. It was back in 2015 when I first heard the mixed version of my own original song "Lisa." I was remodeling one of our rooms in my house and I put "Lisa" on repeat. I probably listened to that song 50 to 100 times a day for a solid week, and it never bored me.

It wasn't an ego thing. In fact, I wasn't particularly proud of it. I am known for a very high, glass-shattering voice, and "Lisa" didn't have any high notes in in. This was actually an acoustic version of one of our (Vendera & Stith) songs, which my songwriting partner tuned down three steps in the studio. Since it was vocally very low in my range, I was afraid people wouldn't like it. (Hmmmm, looks like I was letting fear slip in, another one of those culprits that dim our fire.)

Still, there was something special about that song. It had so much raw emotion that it drew me in as I listened, like a page-turner that a bookworm (I can say that because I am a TOTAL bookworm, ha-ha) cannot put down.

So, what are the most recent music-listening moments for both an album and a single song that you can recall listening to again and again and again?

Once you are certain about your album and song choices, let's move forward in time by a day, week, month, year, however long it took you to realize that you weren't consumed by listening to music anymore.

Can you pinpoint when your passion dulled. Did it occur because you got sidetracked in life with job and family? Or maybe your band broke up and you had no one to practice with? Maybe that affected your enjoyment of listening to music?

Can you recall when music lost its meaning and you quit listening to it every waking moment? What was the last album or song you played over and over again? What year was it when listening to music became a little less important?

Now that we've tackled that beast, let's move on to seek out when you lost the fire for writing music, or recording, or performing.

Was there a time when you were asked to join a band but had to learn 60 songs by the audition, which was still two weeks away. You even knew three-quarters of the songs, but try as you may, you couldn't commit to memory those other songs, so you failed the audition?

Was there a time when you wanted the lead role in a play? Well, you kind of wanted the lead. You dreamed about it, thought about the popularity it would bring you, but you put off remembering the lines and practicing the songs until the final weekend before the audition. Then, when you tried out for the role your mind went blank on stage, you forgot the lyrics, your voice got tight, and you walked off the stage.

What about recording? When did it become so difficult for you? Was there a time when you planned to go into a local recording studio, but you kept putting it off, changing the date, and eventually gave up on the idea of recording your songs because of some irrational excuse you created, such as you felt you weren't ready?

I've been there. I have felt nearly every scenario.

I had a talent for not remembering lyrics when playing in clubs, but only if it was a song I hated to sing. "Addicted to Love" by Robert Palmer comes to mind. A great song for sure, but it didn't interest me. I played keys and sang, and the horn parts in the song I had to play just bored me to death. Since I hated playing the horn parts, it affected my singing, too. I was always bored singing it and could never remember the lyrics.

Or maybe you joined a band that really excited you, but they changed musical directions and it just didn't excite you anymore.

I can relate. This was a difficult memory for me to relive. My passion for playing music dulled around 1993. I quit playing music with an original metal band called AMRA. I was consumed with playing, but our drummer quit to join a country band. I wanted to go out to clubs and watch other bands with my guitarist to find another drummer. He showed up at my house with his girlfriend and blew off our night of seeking a new drummer.

In that moment I felt the flame die, and I told him I was done. I knew inside that I had been bored for months with the music we were writing, but I buried my feelings. I was burned out from even going to rehearsal but hid my boredom.

I mean no disrespect. The guitarist was a great songwriter, but we just had two different writing styles. While I tried to make the best of things and keep going, because we were best friends, in hindsight, I was relieved he had bailed on me that night, because it gave me an excuse to get out of my bored situation.

I quit AMRA and soon after moved in with my then girlfriend/now wife. I told myself that the fire still burned, and this was my chance to be a solo artist. Determined to write and record my own music on my own terms, I bought tons of professional recording equipment, including an Alesis ADAT when they were first released, but I just could never get motivated enough to do anything more than write a song. When it came time to record, I made up a million excuses. "I really don't know how to use this equipment. My microphone isn't good enough. I can't do this without a drum machine. I really need a guitar player."

I just couldn't motivate myself enough to do anything more than hook up all my new, shiny equipment.

Though music was still in my soul, my creative spirit slowly dwindled away that year, and by 1994, I was nothing but a dreamer again.

I know I just depressed all of you, hahaha, but this isn't the end of the story. It was an enlightening gateway to help springboard me back into the zone. Do not take this lightly. Grab your journal and begin recalling every time you can remember being bored with writing, recording, and performing music. Above all, try to pinpoint the first moment that boredom ever set in.

Do NOT move on until you have finished writing out all your "boredom" memories, and thoroughly reviewed each memory, seeking the connection between them all. Once you see the pattern, you can pinpoint what triggers your boredom and puts out your fire.

Don't rush! Look back and think of all those times you noticed the flame growing a little dimmer.

If all this reflection is making you second-guess your true love of music, please don't be alarmed if you feel you've "lost the fire." The fire is still there, it just needs more fuel. I promise that we are working through a process that will bring back your fire!

Once you write down all your "boring" memories and begin to

notice the connections between them, write down a list of what you feel triggered your boredom and dimmed out your creativity spark. Here are a few of my boredom triggers:

- ✓ Songs with simplistic keyboard parts
- ✓ Songs with little vocal harmony
- ✓ Songs with poorly written lyrics
- ✓ Songs that seem to be dragging
- ✓ Unenthusiastic band members

I hope this helped you reveal your boredom triggers. Once you have a list of boredom triggers, we can move onto what triggers our fears.

Fear

Fear, ahhhh, the real musical talent killer. Fear of your skill level, fear of the sound of your own voice, fear of your songwriting abilities, fear of how people will perceive your music, fear of your own musical shadow.

What musicians fail to realize is that we judge ourselves much more harshly than others judge us. We also fail to realize that music is an expression of each individual's soul. Therefore, it stands to reason that since we all have a right to our own voice, to our own musical expression through any musical instrument, a right to express ourselves as we musically see fit, then ALL music has a place.

Every song you write is YOUR interpretation of your emotions, memories, experiences in the world surrounding you. Every cover song you perform is YOUR interpretation of what the original artist is feeling in the context of that song.

At the core of your musical DNA, you are your own individualistic artist, your own unique performer, your own one-of-kind songwriter, therefore NOBODY can do YOU better than YOU. In fact, a great reminder to yourself is to recite the following on a daily basis:

I AM MY OWN BEST ARTIST

Too many musicians become too self-conscious about their own abilities. I understand your fear and self-doubt. I know that the fear can paralyze you. It has happened to me.

I can remember my sophomore year when the high school marching band was at a band competition. We had several hours of downtime before we had to march on the field. I was hanging out on the school bus listening to the radio with my best friend. My favorite song at the time, "Oh Sheila," by Ready for the World, was playing on the radio. I began to sing along, like I always do.

My buddy turned to me with a smug look and said, "Shut it, James. You can't sing."

I was 14 at the time. I was so overcome by fear of what people would think of my singing that I quit singing for nearly two years.

I also recall my senior year when someone found lyrics to a song I was writing in my notebook. He looked at me, snickering as he said, "Great lyrics," sarcastically adding, "They're *really* good."

It upset me, and though I shrugged it off and continued to write lyrics, for a short time I became very guarded about sharing them with anyone.

I was also actively playing the club circuit my senior year in high school. I had gotten over my fears of what people thought of me. But I recall playing one gig where the singer from another band had come to watch us play. He was very nice and said I had a good voice. But as the night progressed and he became inebriated, he pulled me to the side during a break and said, "James, you're a really good singer, but you'll never be as good as me."

Though it negatively affected me the rest of the night, I was reminded later that he was very belligerent and never had a kind word to say about any other musician. So the fear melted quickly.

But wait, there's more, and it will shock you. Do you remember my story about "Sweating Bullets"? That night was the highlight of that band for me. I loved that band. I loved the players, Scott, David, Lonnie, and Jeff. I loved the songs "Sweating Bullets," "Cries in the Night," and "Desiré," to name a few, and I loved the band name, Chained Angel. Above all, I had a great songwriting partner in Scott Stith (and all these years later, we're still writing together).

However, the night didn't end well. My best friend had just moved back from Hollywood, and he came to watch us play. At the end of the gig, before he left, he said, "You guys sounded great ... but you're not happy."

I chuckled and said, "I am very happy."

He smiled and rebuked my words. "No, you're not. You were only meant to be in a band with me. Now that I am back, we need to start another band."

His words weighed heavy on my heart for weeks. I developed self-doubt, began to believe what others had said, that the guys in Chained Angel were too young and too green. I began to wonder if our songs were any good. In the end, it ate at me like a disease and led me to quitting Chained Angel and forming AMRA with Matt, though I knew it was the wrong thing to do. While I loved Matt like a brother, and still do, it was my own fears that caused the breakup of an amazing five-piece.

As you can see, we all experience fear and doubt at some point in our musical lives, and if we let it, it can be the ruination of our musical creativity.

While I DO understand self-doubt, it does NOT have to define you! We can begin to redefine ourselves in a positive light if we unveil these fear triggers. Once we see what causes our fear, we can face it and eliminate it.

Your assignment for this section of the chapter is to look back on your life and face your fears by recalling those memories where your fire dimmed due to your own fears. Once you have recalled those memories, you can discover the connections, those common threads between them, those triggers that incite fear.

Make a new memory list for those fear triggers. Here are some of mine:

- ✓ Negative criticism from other musicians
- ✓ Doubting my singing abilities
- ✓ Fear of what others think of my voice
- ✓ Fear of what others will think of my lyrics
- ✓ Doubting my songwriting skills
- ✓ Wondering what people think of me as a performer

And the biggest fear I have, which I didn't even realize until my guitarist Scott Stith pointed out that he had it, too:

- ✓ The fear of the song recording being perfect!!!

We both have over-analyzed every step of recording, every vocal tone, every guitar strum to the point of recording one simple part again and again and again because we felt it was never good enough, that "it was never perfect."

There is no such thing as "perfect," because we all have different views of perfection. What one person might view as perfection in a song someone else would view as imperfection.

You know what? That is okay, because this is why we all are drawn to different styles of music. Music is a matter of personal taste, and regardless of your personal tastes, an artist who is expressing their personal tastes can be perfect in the moment of expressing their own creativity while writing, recording, and performing the song.

Hang on to that thought! Allow yourself to express your inner musings, allow yourself to be "perfect in the moment," and then no fear can bind you!

NONE of my fears, or your fears, hold true. Music is art in the ear of the beholder and "perfection" is a thing of the moment. If you sing and play with your heart—provided you have practiced enough to learn your skill—then that snapshot in time during that recording, during that performance, will be perfect in representing that moment in time.

Just remember that the things we fear and overanalyze are typically over-exaggerated by our own fears. But in the end, there is no proof that those fears are valid!

Once you've finished this chapter and complete all of Part Two of *Mind Over Music*, I HIGHLY suggest you take a week off from reading this book. This process is a lot to mentally take in and accept. We can be guarded at times, so putting the book down for a week in favor of reviewing your memories and lists may open you up a bit more and allow you to remember other key points in your life that related to your musical past.

During the following week, add more notes, add more memories, and make sure you've made a thorough list of your motivational sparks of creativity, your boredom triggers, and your fear triggers.

These lists will help you rekindle your flame to bring you closer to music as well as help you avoid slipping back into negative patterns that can smother your creativity, drive, and focus. You need to know that you do NOT have to keep clinging to triggers in your life that create boredom and fear.

Spend this week in serious self-reflection so that you are prepared to move forward, fueled by your creative sparks while seeking out new creative sparks, and avoiding those boredom and fear triggers, while acknowledging any new triggers that occur.

In the three steps we'll soon learn, you'll be able to apply what you've learned thus far to make the road to your musical success a much smoother ride.

PART THREE

Fueling the Fire

NOW THAT YOU'RE ARMED with lots of information concerning your musical past, you have the tools to begin the three-step process with an almost clean slate. You've reminisced and recalled all those past times when you were so on fire for music that you felt it vibrating all the way down into your bones. I bet those memories put a huge smile on your face.

You've also faced those times when the flame dimmed. You've dug deep to discover what bored you or let fear settle in, causing you to lose interest in music or doubt your musical abilities. Learning the emotional pros and cons that connected or disconnected you from music is a tool to help you overcome all negative obstacles and enable you to rekindle your motivational spark of creativity. You now have the tools to annihilate procrastination and get back to the grind of creating and living music.

Fueling the fire is easy. Simply make sure that you are actively doing fun tasks daily that relate to music, those moments that involve your passion and trigger your motivational sparks of creativity, while consciously avoiding those situations that trigger boredom and fear.

This might seem easier said than done, but I promise that it IS easier done! It is MUCH easier to live in inspiration than to be paralyzed by boredom and fear. You only THINK it is easier to avoid your creative side. But once you've taken the first few steps to get out of that procrastination rut of doing nothing and back to doing something, you will be amazed at how easy it is to exist in a state of constant creative flow!

Good news! You've already taken those first few steps toward your musical success drive and creative freedom by discovering your motivational sparks of creativity and your boredom and fear triggers. Now we can put those initial steps into play within the *Mind Over Music* three-step formula. It will flow so easily that it will feel like it is a natural part of you. You won't feel like there are tons of things you need to do to reach the next level of success.

Now that you've laid the foundation, it's time to begin building your musical legacy by choosing your first goal and stating your intention.

Chapter Six
SETTING YOUR FIRST GOAL
(Step One—Setting Your Intention)

We've reached the first step toward turning you into one awesome music-making machine!!!!

It's great that you've reviewed your life and made a list of your motivational sparks of creativity, as well as discovered boredom and fear triggers. That is amazing progress. Working through that entire process has already affected your views of music and stimulated your mind in ways you're not even aware of yet. Please note, this list isn't final. You can add to it at any time, and most likely, you WILL be adding more memories as they unfold. If any other memory pops into your mind, any motivational sparks of creativity, boredom triggers, fear triggers, write them down!!!

I know I sound like a broken record (I slipped that musical reference in here on purpose, ha-ha), but I wanted to state one final time just how important it is for you to do the memory exercises to lay the groundwork for what is to come.

Now, onto Step One, THE GOAL or the INTENTION!!! FYI, to me, the words "Goal" and "Intention" are interchangeable. It is simply a reference to what you wish to accomplish, so please note that any time you see either word in this book, I am referring to that which you intend to accomplish.

Now it is time to choose your first important musical goal/set your first intention. Choose your first musical project to tackle based on what will excite you and give you great pleasure. Is it one song, your next album, or putting a band together to write music? What is it? What musical project would YOU like to tackle first? Whatever it is, write it down!

No, seriously, WRITE IT DOWN! In Your *Mind Over Music* workbook, I want you to go to a blank page and at the top, write,

MY MUSIC GOAL IS _____.
I INTEND TO ACCOMPLISH THIS GOAL BY _____.

Yes, we need a date. Setting a deadline creates a mental priority, which we will cover more in Step Three. That is why you must write down your goal and set the deadline.

I am very proud of you! Just knowing that you picked your goal and you WANT to set an intention toward accomplishing something music related tells me that music is encoded in your DNA and is a strong part of your genetic programming. Actually, music (aka "vibration") is coded into ALL of our DNA, because we are vibration. However, since you're reading this book, I know you're feel the calling of song a little more than my son, Ryan.

You see, Ryan really loves music. He loves listening to it, and he even tackled bass guitar for a while. But Ryan REALLY LOVES fishing; he cannot get enough of it. It is all he thinks about. When he is fishing, he does like to listen to music. So he does have a connection to his musical DNA, but it isn't one of his main genetic programs. He has the DNA, but he doesn't have the full calling. His DNA is more in tune with fishing.

Since YOUR passion is music, it is time to break the code.

I truly believe, whoops, I mean I truly KNOW that if you have any inkling of a desire to play in a band, perform on stage, write a song, and release that song, then you were not only encoded with the love of music, but your DNA was also programmed to create music. Your cellular musical program is up-to-date. Time to start running the program, so to speak.

The first step to running the program is figuring out what "viruses" are infecting your program. The biggest virus is procrastination, spread by, you guessed it, fear or boredom, which is blocking you from finishing songs, recording songs, or keeping you from forming your band. Procrastination IS the virus that results from fear or loss of interest. To conquer that virus, you must decide if the spreading of the virus is from boredom or fear.

Guess what? We already figured it out! It is all those boredom and fear triggers. Since you know what is keeping you from performing, writing, and recording, we CAN address each trigger and remove them from our life.

Some of you might balk at me for making you face the truth, and you may even say that you have no boredom or fear triggers, that your problem is simply work- and family-related. This is not true. Yes, some things in life, like putting food on the table, might come first, BUT it will never be at the cost of your motivational spark of creativity. Those who told you that you cannot play music and have a "real" career have lied to you. If you have the fire, you WILL ALWAYS find a way to work music into your daily life!

FYI, whenever I begin writing a new book, I either already have or immediately do put into practice the techniques that I am writing about. *Mind Over Music* was no different. I tried it out on myself and a friend, who wishes to remain anonymous Let's call him Chris. Chris, who is in a country band. He really has a great time with his band. They play out once or twice a month, though he wishes it were more. He also wishes he had more time to practice. But by the time he drives to and from work, 30 minutes each way, then helps with his kids, he says he's just too tired to schedule more than one practice a week and two gigs per month. He dreams about it a lot, though.

Chris asked me for help. He said he was afraid that music was over for him and it really depressed him. So we went through the entire

Mind Over Music process. He sought out his motivational sparks of creativity, and he searched for boredom and fear triggers, but he felt like he came up empty. He believed my approach was a failure.

About two weeks after he created his *Mind Over Music* workbook, he had a dream. He called me up to tell me about it. He said the dream was more of a memory of him at ten years old getting up on stage and playing a song on the banjo at one of his older brother's gigs. His brother was an amazing banjo player, but Chris always felt inferior to his brother, so he picked up acoustic guitar instead, and in his teens he started a modern country band. That was twenty years ago.

His dream was emotionally vivid. He felt the intense energy and fire he had inside him when he was playing that banjo, and he suddenly realized all the self-doubt that he had about his playing. He was always worried and stressed about how he would be compared to his brother, though his brother never made him feel that way. He said he woke up in a sweat and grabbed his *Mind Over Music* workbook and started writing it all down.

His memory made him realize that his true passion was bluegrass, not country. But his self-conscious doubts held him back. Once he realized the issue, he knew why he wasn't booking more gigs, why he wasn't practicing more, why he was too tired at night to play his guitar. He was uninspired because he wasn't playing bluegrass. He was bored with modern country, and his own fear of playing his true chosen instrument and style of music left him settling for something similar but not his goal.

Things unfolded fast. Now that he was armed with these new tools, he told his band how he felt and that he wanted to start a bluegrass band so he could play banjo and have a harmony quartet in the band. Much to his surprise, three out of the four members had felt the same way. The drummer admitted that he was bored because he always wanted to be in a rock band. So, with encouragement from all the members, the drummer left to join a rock band and the rest formed a bluegrass quartet, with Chris on banjo and lead vocals.

He told me that the fire he had at ten years old is back. The band was just as excited and had come up with a plan to rehearse Monday through Thursday. They started looking for and booking gigs every weekend. Chris loaded his iPhone with all his favorite bluegrass songs to motivate him while he drove to and from work. He hired a banjo teacher to improve his skills. He even started writing music.

Together, this new band set a goal to work hard and play as many gigs as possible, and they're already being offered gigs at venues that hadn't hired them before. They're also working on their first album of original songs and have already started the recording process. Mind you, this happened in a matter of weeks!

Chris is now living and breathing music with new excitement, and he told me that his biggest fan is his older brother.

You see, once you've discovered the motivational sparks of creativity, faced those boredom and fear triggers as nothing more than minor setbacks that can be eliminated, and set an intention, you are well on your way to music success.

Back to Step One. You MUST decide on your first goal right now!!!

Tell me again, what is your first intention?

Unsure? Well, let's pick one together. Actually, I picked mine a few weeks ago. My music goal is to release one solo single. I intend to release this song by the end of this year. Wow, sounds like I'm being lazy. Actually, I'm not. By applying the techniques in *Mind Over Music*, I've already written a parody song for Sean Daniel Media, which we are recording and using for a funny music video for this Spring, and I've recorded Extreme Scream 3, an audio instruction program with rock and metal songs for singers. ES3 was supposed to be recorded THREE YEARS AGO. But I knocked it out in ONE DAY when I started writing *Mind Over Music*.

So my goal for one solo song is my simple goal for making myself happy. Who knows how many songs I'll release now that my fire is back.

It is important to note that I have thought a lot about this goal. I followed my heart to let it tell me just what kind of song I needed to write. My heart told me that I want to write a song all by myself that is mainly piano and vocals with string orchestration and massive vocal harmonies, with every part played by me, just to prove that *Mind Over Music* works.

Now that I have set a goal and intend to release it by the end of the year, what do I need to do to make this goal a reality? Well, you really do not need to worry about this in Step One, as these answers will unfold in the next two steps. But, since you asked, I know I haven't really played piano in years, so common sense tells me that I need to work on my piano chops. I also need to study up on string orchestration. I would also say I need to write a song, hahaha, but I swear the moment I set this intention, tons of piano ideas were already popping into my head. See how quick that worked! I set the intention and BAM, I am already being flooded.

I also know that for the vocal approach I am hearing in my head I will need a specific microphone and preamp, too. This isn't me making excuses. I have a mic and preamp now, so nothing will hold me back from recording the song. However, in my mind, I want to write and release a song similar to "She's Gone" by Steelheart. I want to release a song as epic as that song. That's why I want a different mic, one more suitable for a dynamic range. But I don't want to just run out and buy them. I know I am covered regardless, but I want to see what my intention will do to align my thought process to receiving the microphone and preamp I have in mind.

Now that I have an intention, I want to make sure I have the burning desire. I've got to find that burning desire. And since I know that I've faced the fact that I don't have the same burning desire to listen to music over and over again as I did in my teens, I need some stimulation to rekindle that flame. It just so happens that I have the perfect way to do that so that it instills my intention into every cell of my body. I call this my Music Caffeine Playlist.

I've previously mentioned this, but it deserves repeating. When I was a teen, I could listen to cassette tapes over and over and over again. Somewhere along the way, I lost that fire. But I recently found a way to bring it back. I revisited all those songs that got my adrenaline racing in my youth, the songs on albums that I couldn't wait to hear again, the songs that I could remember every vocal lick, every drum fill, every bass line.

Once I revisited those specific songs, I made a playlist of songs for a "30-minute mix tape" filled with songs to get my blood pumping and heart racing, including "She's Gone" as the mix tape ender, since I was planning to write an epic song similar to it. My Music Caffeine Playlist is like a shot of adrenaline when I listen to it. I play it when I am running on the treadmill. I play it when I am writing a book. I play it whenever I am driving in my car. And with every song I hear on my playlist, I think about my intention. This playlist gets my heart pumping because it is full of high energy, loud, fast-paced rock songs ending with the piano song.

What are you waiting for? Why haven't you made your Music Caffeine Playlist yet? Better get started. If I may interject here, I am an avid fan of Joe Vitale. I probably have read just about everything he's written. And as I write this, I remember that he released an audio program called "Music Caffeine" that helped to energize your body. So props to Joe. I didn't mean to steal your name, but there really isn't any other name for such a cool playlist, hahaha.

Now that you've created your playlist, here is a little bonus tip to enhance the effectiveness of your listening sessions. As you listen to the songs, you can enhance the amount of mental and physical energy you build simply by panting in and out as you listen to the beat of the drum, with every beat resulting in one inhalation and one exhalation for a two-count per beat. A half hour of panting and high energy music will make you feel great, energized, and even healthier. This is a little trick I learned from attending a few holotropic breathwork workshops.

Please note, you should NOT attempt to pant for the entire thirty minutes. This is an extreme physical process that requires time to improve your breathing stamina. You do NOT want to do this behind the wheel of a car. It can make you light-headed until you master the ability to pant for longer periods of time in rhythm with the beat of the music.

To recap:
1. Pick your one goal. Set your intention to accomplish that goal. You MUST also set a timeline. Get out a calendar and write down a day, whether it is next week, a month from now, or right before next Christmas. Set that intention and date it!
2. Make your Music Caffeine Playlist. Fill it full of thirty minutes worth of the songs that once coursed through your veins, high-energy songs that you played over and over and over again. If in your intention you have one song that you can relate to the type of song or album you want to write, add it as the very last song on your playlist. It is the cap-off to the energy. Listen to this playlist as often as possible and ALWAYS think about your goal as you listen. You CAN think about the steps it takes to reach that goal, like rehearsing, going into the studio, etc., as long as you do not attach any fear or doubt to those steps or question how to make the steps work. We'll cover this as we proceed into the other steps. To increase your energy during your Music Caffeine Playlist sessions, learn to pant in rhythm with the bass drum.

Make sense so far? Good. If you've set your intention and created your Music Caffeine Playlist, you are well on your way to finding your FLOW. Once you live in flow with music, you will be able to slip in and out of what we call "the zone" as often as required.

DO NOT move on to Step Two until you've completed Step One.

Ah, I see that you have completed Step One. You're feeling the fire getting hotter again!

Great!

It is now time to flip the page and continue this journey!!!

Chapter Seven
CLEARING THE PATH
(Step Two—Clearing Negative Beliefs)

NOW THAT YOU ARE focused on your goal, you've set a date for completing your intention, and you're energizing your mind and body every day with your Music Caffeine Playlist, you need to revisit that list of boredom and fear triggers so you can apply key tactics to remove those triggers from your path. Just because you've made the list of triggers and now know what bores you and makes you doubt yourself doesn't mean you've cleared the path to success.

Those triggers still exist, and knowing you should avoid them doesn't mean you WILL avoid them. However, Step Two in the *Mind Over Music* method WILL teach you to eliminate those triggers!

Let's begin by rereading our two lists of triggers. As you reread your lists, replay in your mind how each trigger affected you. If new triggers come to mind, please add them to your lists, no matter how small or insignificant it might be. If you recall a period in your life when you were supposed to learn a new song by the weekend, but you were binge-watching the first season of a TV show to prepare for the upcoming Season 2, that IS a boredom trigger. Although it seems insignificant and not a roadblock in your path to learning that song by the weekend, write it down!!! Seeming insignificant doesn't mean it is insignificant.

Every time you were lazy and avoided music, no matter how

seemingly small or insignificant, WRITE IT DOWN! Write down ANY negative memory that comes to mind that is not in your *Mind Over Music* workbook. Record ANY memory you've ever had concerning music and your musical abilities.

FYI, this goes for the fear triggers, too. Dig deep to find triggers you didn't even know you had.

One fear trigger that JUST popped up in my mind as I was writing this was a time over ten years ago when I was jealous of a fellow vocal coach who was on the road touring with a huge rock band, making tons of money, and having a blast on the road. I thought, "Why does HE get to do that and not me?" I instantly knew that this memory was a fear trigger, not plain jealousy. At that moment in my life, I was comparing my level of success to someone I truly admired who has been teaching far longer than I have. My fear was thinking I'd never reach that level of vocal coaching success. Now I know to face the fear and let it go.

In a sense, boredom triggers and fear triggers are road signs to help us overcome our musical laziness and doubt. It is how we process them—whether we cling to them or let them go—that will affect our musical success. All those moments of procrastination and all those self-doubts are simply your ego talking, the part of you that questions everything you do.

On the other hand, your pure creative source, or your intuition, is the part of your mind that gifts you with all your song ideas, helps you to find your flow, takes you to the path that leads to being in the zone. It doesn't get in your creative way, like the ego does.

Yes, the ego can be a pest. It knows when you aren't into the music, so it whispers for you to be lazy, to lie on the couch watching Netflix when you could be writing another song. It whispers those little lies of self-doubt when it isn't fully invested in your musical dreams. It enjoys whispering all your doubts, fears, and false beliefs to you. If it can, it will get you to believe every false thing about yourself. It will also question every step of your process, which is where those fears kick in.

But it also knows what drives you. It knows what excites you and drives your passion—and what bores you. When you begin to flow with creativity, the ego will let loose its reins and allow the motivational spark of creativity (which comes from your subconscious, or for those of you who understand the deeper connection, the superconscious) to take the lead.

That is why Step One is so important. You need to set a goal to figure out what it is you really want to do with music. Maybe you're in an Aerosmith tribute band because you can imitate Steven Tyler. While it is fun, you'd prefer to be writing and singing dance music and doing a bit of rapping. But you avoid it because the live music scene where you live doesn't call for many dance bands. Bam, that's the ego keeping you from your true passion.

You need to follow your gut! What is your musical DNA telling you? In the end, remember, there's nothing wrong with any style of music. If you follow your calling you will succeed. If you're bored being a rocker and want to be a pop artist/rapper, then DO IT! QUIT worrying about what people will think! QUIT being bored in a band that doesn't excite you! QUIT being in fear of changing your musical style!

Regardless of what is triggering your procrastination, whether you've been lazy due to boredom with your current musical situation or you're fearful about your abilities, the first step toward eliminating these triggers is to QUIT thinking of music as a side hobby. It is part of your DNA! It is part of what defines you.

Learn to let it define you wherever you are. When I worked construction, I was a "construction worker," but when people would ask me, "What do you do for a living," I'd reply, "I am a singer," because I am always a singer. It is part of my DNA.

Though we've thoroughly covered what triggers us to become bored and lazy and unveiled our fears, we need to define them into sentences that pertain to our current situation. Because, now that you've set a goal and set your intention, I PROMISE that new fears will arise. So, repeat your goal from Step One aloud and then allow your mind to think of all the negative scenarios that could create boredom and fear to block you from your goal.

Here are a few that come to mind when I think about my goal:

- ✓ I won't be able to write an impressive piano piece.
- ✓ I'm not good at orchestrating string parts.
- ✓ I've too many ideas of how I want the vocals to sound. I don't know which is best.
- ✓ I am not sure I'll get that new mic and preamp in time.
- ✓ I really want to catch up on *The Walking Dead*.
- ✓ There's a new *Stargate* website, and now I want to binge watch all the shows.
- ✓ I want to read the new *Shannara* book series, but I need to reread the series first.
- ✓ Recording is great, but I could use that time to teach more students.

So, you see, those triggers can creep in at any time, brand new ones, too! For example, if you've set a goal to record an album and release it in six months, and you have NEVER recorded anything in your life, some of the boredom and fear triggers concerning the *ifs*, *whens*, *hows*, *whys*, and *whats* of songwriting and recording could include:

- ✓ I've never recorded before, so I probably won't be any good at recording.
- ✓ Maybe six months isn't enough time.
- ✓ I don't have any extra time in my busy schedule to record.
- ✓ I don't even know when I'll have time to write a song.
- ✓ How can I raise the money to record?
- ✓ I don't have a good amp.

- ✓ I'll be ready if I spend the next few months watching how-to videos on YouTube.

While those are all fear-based triggers, you could have boredom triggers, too, such as:

- ✓ Before I start recording this album, I should watch every music documentary out there to learn what makes rock stars tick.
- ✓ I'll be inspired to write if I go kayaking this weekend instead of recording.
- ✓ I really need a nap before I can get started recording.

You can see how these boredom triggers are nothing more than excuses, pulling you away from writing and recording, BUT you can also see that signs of boredom could also be a side-effect of your fears.

This is when you must be 100% sure that the goals you set are exactly what you want to create musically. If not, then those bouts of procrastination, when you're kayaking instead of recording, are because you're not writing the music that is in your DNA.

Doubts and excuses are two sides of the same coin:

- ✓ "How will I pay for the recording?"
- ✓ "I don't have a drummer."
- ✓ "I am too busy at work to make time for writing and recording."
- ✓ "I will record my record, but I need a few more years of practice first."

The excuses are endless. BUT all those doubts and excuses are based on your perceived realty, everything in your life that seems set in stone.

However, the ego isn't all bad. Yeah, it will make you doubt yourself, make you lazy, give you all kinds of excuses to avoid your musical calling. But it also can be swayed in our favor.

It's easy to sway that ego to let go of those negative beliefs and clear the path. Joe already told you how to do it. To sway your ego in your favor, just ask yourself,

"Where's the proof?"

There isn't any!!!

I made you discover all these triggers for a reason. When a musician who is procrastinating is forced to look at their situation to figure out "why" they aren't getting things done, the excuses pop up, and as usual, they are based on boredom and fears. Take, for example, the excuse of "writer's block."

Writer's block doesn't exist. There is NO writer's block. There is only writer's flow. Think of a waterfall. Sometimes it is small, sometimes large. Think of a faucet that drips. It is always drip-drip-dripping. But turn it on and the stream is strong. When the road to your goal isn't clear, when it is full of negative beliefs, your flow is slow; it just drip-drip-drips. That's when the excuses start flowing more than your creativity, and as you know, excuses are caused by boredom and/or fear. An excuse is nothing more than validation of a trigger.

When the creative faucet is on, it gushes. Excuses slow up that faucet. Any excuse for not finishing a song or forming a band is ONLY an excuse and holds no real power!

Where's the Proof?

If you want to delete all those negative excuses, overcome your bouts of boredom, and get rid of your fears, you CAN! If you can perceive it, you WILL achieve it! if you can perceive overcoming every roadblock and achieving your goal, then you can, plain and simple! No lie. I know, I know, you're looking for some "golden key" to eliminating them from your mind. Well, you should know that triggers will always arise. New ones will be born with every goal you set. BUT you can simply accept them as fact or question their validity by looking at every fear and doubt and excuse and saying aloud, "Where's the proof?"

If your mind doesn't even recognize there is a doubt, then no doubt will exist.

For example, many times at the gym I've grabbed one 50-pound dumbbell and one 55-pound dumbbell for a dumbbell press and not even realized it. Yet I didn't notice the 5-pound difference as I did my set, and only discovered it later. Then I could feel the weight shifting, one side a little heavier than the other, causing a struggle to balance it out. Worse, I might let a fear settle in and think that I can only handle the 50-pound weights. Yet a moment earlier I didn't even notice it and was successful with 55 pounds.

Here's another example. One of my favorite games with my vocal students is to ask them what their highest comfortable singing note is before we begin an exercise. When we begin to vocalize, I tell them where we're starting, for example, on a middle C. In actuality, I am starting three notes higher, on D#. Once the singer has reached their highest note (the note they told me they could reach) right before we attempt it, I say, "Okay, three more notes to go until we reach your highest note. How is your voice feeling?"

They always respond positively. "My voice feels good. No strain at all."

When I get them to their perceived highest note (which is now actually three notes higher), they seem to struggle a little bit. They believe that is the top of their range, so they allow the doubt and fear to creep in. Yet I encourage them, tell them they can do it. I have them focus, and if the student reaches the note with no strain, I ask them to go one note above their "highest note."

Whether they stop at their perceived highest note or go one more note, they ended up increasing their perceived vocal range by three to four notes higher than what they felt they could do.

This is the power of mental choice. You can trick your own mind easily, even if you are consciously aware that you're tricking your mind. If you doubt your abilities, you simply ask, "Where's the proof?" Begin asking that simple question any time you feel the fear or notice you're becoming lazy.

Boredom trigger: "I should binge watch these recording videos over the next few days before I start recording."

Reality: Where's the proof you need to watch those videos? Let's skip the videos, start recording, and see what happens.

Fear trigger: "I'll never finish this song because I cannot hit that high note I hear in my head."

Reality: Where's the proof? Keep aiming for that note until you get it!

Utilizing "Where's the proof?" will make for better practice, better rehearsals, better shows, and faster output.

Whisper Words

I've got one more amazing little tactic for you to eliminate those triggers. It is what I use to overcome my fears. I call them whisper words. You might be familiar with the terms "mantras" and "affirmations." Whisper words are basically the same concept, but I liken it to a tiny voice inside your head whispering short sentences to encourage you to overcome and conquer.

I swear I'm not crazy (well, maybe a little), but I've heard whisper words all my life. These have always been short sentences of warning like,

Don't take this exit, as mentioned in *Unleash Your Creative Mindset.*

Or,

"*It's your time,*" as mentioned in *Raise Your Voice.*

Want the full story on the two examples of whisper words? Read my books, hahaha.

Okay, I'll share a few stories so you know just how crazy I am, hahaha. I began to consciously take notice that whisper words were popping into my mind on their own in my early twenties. The first time it was a warning to prevent me from a car wreck. Other times words of encouragement were whispered to me. Whenever it happened I almost felt as if there were two of me. The second version of me, the one that was whispering, was looking at me from outside my body.

When I realized that it was my subconscious reaching out to me to guide me and protect me at times, I was able to take control of my whisper words. I began to string short sentences together and whisper them to myself as I pictured the second me whispering the words of encouragement. This is a technique I still use to this day whenever I am writing a book or performing on a television show. It is an extreme motivator when I visualize observing what "Jaime" is accomplishing at that moment.

For example, whenever I am working on song lyrics and feel a momentary loss of concentration, I use this technique to get back into the zone. I step outside myself to view "Jaime" in the moment and whisper words like, *"You're almost done"* or *"What rhymes with pain?"* I do it to stimulate my focus and encourage my mind to find the right word to finish the line.

Whisper words have become natural to me because I started using them when I was five and never really stopped. As a child, I had no neighbors to play with from five years old until second grade, so I created two make-believe friends to keep me company. I became so accustomed to carrying on full conversations with myself that it felt like a natural part of life.

I became very intuitive with it, as if I were honing a specific skill to allow my intuition to speak to me. Eventually, my make-believe friends faded and were replaced by a carbon copy of myself.

Whenever I was nervous during school for a test, such as a spelling quiz, second Jaime would whisper words of encouragement. If I couldn't remember the spelling of a word, I'd listen for that soft voice and imagine my carbon copy appearing next to me to whisper the answer in my ear.

Indeed, it helped, because I already knew the answers; I was just drawing them out of me.

I also used this technique to overcome stage fright when I started playing in clubs at 16 years old. My whisper words of encouragement for the stage were, *"They love you."*

Now, whenever I perform on television, shattering glass with my voice, I hear, *"Watch it explode."*

Granted, some whisper words still come to me out of thin air, like the time I was teaching a class of vocal coaches and doctors how to scream without hurting your voice. As I took the podium for my two-hour class, I became so nervous that my throat went dry in the first two minutes of speaking. I had a fear of being judged by all the amazing coaches and doctors in the audience.

Then a voice whispered, *"You got this!"* That is all it took for me to regain my composure and have a great two-hour class!

New whisper words fill my mind all the time, whether I consciously create them or they subconsciously appear.

You got this!

Time to get up!

You need more water!

As you now see, I've had many instances where whisper words came to me out of thin air, while other whisper words are short sentences I created to prepare for any given situation. I'd then mentally repeat my whisper words to myself as needed. I guess you could say that whisper words, whether formed subconsciously or consciously, are MY form of positive affirmations.

Lately I've been hearing a tiny whisper at night as I drift off to sleep that says, *"Show me."* These whisper words were not of my conscious making, but I already know what they mean. When Joe first told me this was my book to write before he came on board, I was slow to begin. Hmmm, sounds like the triggers were setting in. In actuality, I was fearful. Here was one of my idols saying that he would co-author a book with me. How amazing is that!!!

Then I began to worry about how to write it so that once he read it, it could easily be turned into a co-author joint venture. So, for the first few weeks, I wrote next to nothing. But every night, a voice whispered, *"Show me."*

I finally realized that I needed to write, to show that I had a goal, that no fear would stop me, that I was taking action. I wasn't showing "anyone" anything. I was procrastinating on writing this book until I realized that my newest whisper words were encouraging me to not think, just write. Write I did, and those two whisper words stopped being whispered to me once I took action to finish this book!

Whisper words will work for you, too. They do not need to be repeated all day long like an affirmation. Repeat them as needed. Some other whisper words you can use are:

> *Keep going.*
> *You're doing great.*
> *You got this.*
> *Just one more time.*
> *That sounds amazing.*
> *That was beautiful.*

You can create your own short sentences to function as your personal whisper words to use whenever you feel like those boredom and fear triggers are taking control. Study yourself; when you realize you've made an excuse, use those whisper words to help you flip the switch back to your favor again. Ask, "Where's the proof?" In fact, turn those into whisper words. Hear that tiny voice whisper, *"Where's the proof?"* to clear those negative doubts.

Before ending this step, you should know that clearing negativity from your life will be a continual process. There will always be outside influence from others or situations that can cause those old triggers—and even new triggers—to arise. Joe taught me this, which is why he is in a continual state of clearing, using the ancient technique known as Ho'oponopono, not only for himself but also for anyone and everyone that he thinks to clear. His techniques for clearing affect your entire being (and those around you) and are not just music related. I HIGHLY suggest you read both, *At Zero* and *Zero Limits* by Dr. Joe Vitale to learn more about the clearing process!

Using the techniques you've mastered so far in this book will help you take action much more quickly and effectively than you can imagine, which brings us to our last step: Time to take action!!!

Chapter Eight
REACHING THE FINISH LINE
(Step Three—Taking Action)

WOO-HOO, WE'VE REACHED the final step of this amazing journey. Now it's time to work toward that finish line. Now it's time to get to work!!!

Surely you knew you were going to have to work hard to reach your goal. Surely you didn't think that it was going to be as easy as setting an intention, eliminating a few fears, and hopping off the boredom train and you'd magically arrive at the finish line?

Where would the fun it that be?!?!?

Nope, you need to help the process by working for it. But I PROMISE that it will be a fun-filled ride. I mean, music is fun, isn't it! That's a statement, not a question. Even if you feel like some of the fun died along the way, I am betting you feel the fun returning. You're neck deep in this program so far, so I KNOW that you know that I know you are noticing some major positive changes occurring.

- Some of the love you've lost for listening to music is returning.
- You've already weeded out nearly all the excuses you've made to avoid creating music.
- You're feeling the fire again.
- You've noticed that that hour of band practice that you

used to dread is now turning into a three-hour joy ride that flies by like it lasted only minutes.
- You're over your so-called writer's block and have written more songs in three days than you have in the last three years.

Shall I go on? You fill in the blanks. :)

Now that you're noticing changes, it's time to focus on what else you can physically and consciously do to help accomplish your goal by your deadline. In all honesty, I never refer to my deadlines as "deadlines." For years, I've jokingly thought of them as "lifelines."

In truth, that is what they are, because your goal date is the day that you've set to bring your creative expression to life. Whether it is a song, a full album, or a band playing their first gig, the moments of music are your children. As you work toward that goal, thinking of your "lifeline," you are in the birthing period. You're nurturing your creativity, feeding it so that it grows, feeding it with your heart, mind, and soul to assure that your creation, this child, is a healthy child, and once this child is ready to be born, it is introduced to the world on the day of its "lifeline."

Once your child is born, you feel a great sense of pride and love for this song, this album, this band, and you name the child—you give it a song name, an album name, a band name. You created this child. This is a child born of your motivational spark of creativity. What an amazing act of love!

Now that I've gotten all lovey-dovey on you, haha, let's look at ways to help nurture this "child" along to its birth. There are many ways to work toward your goal. Let's start with defining your get-up-and-go moment.

Defining Your Get-Up-and-Go Moment

I am a reader's reader. I LOVE to read and absorb tons of information, especially information that motivates me toward success. Lately, I've been seeing a lot of books pushing "The 5 a.m. Morning," which is a concept that states you can get more done if you start your day at 5 a.m.

I must agree; it's a beautiful concept. I generally start my day at 4:30 a.m., waking up and heading to the gym. I work out for 60 to 90 minutes, head home, take my shower, go over my vocal exercises, answer all my emails, write for at least 30 minutes on any book I am working on as I eat a quick breakfast, and review my lesson schedule for the day. I accomplish all this by 8 a.m.

WOW, that is amazing. But it is amazing because it works for me. I define early morning as my get-up-and-go moment, that moment my mind and body say, "Okay, let's get it done!" It's the perfect moment to enthusiastically begin my personal tasks that have to do with keeping my voice and body in shape. It also seems to be the best time for me to write books. By 8 a.m., once I've reviewed my schedule, I know I can continue working on my book or switch to filming videos for my online school. Early morning is my creative flow for these projects.

But it's not my creative flow time for songwriting or recording.

I've tried to write songs early and record early. While I am not triggered by fear or boredom not to write and record in the morning (and it has nothing to do with my voice not being ready), I have simply learned over the years that my get-up-and-go moment that allows me to slip into the zone is later in the evening.

For me, when the sun begins to go down and I can dim the lights in my studio, it creates an ambience of flow. I can feel it. My creative juices start flowing, my voice feels stronger and stronger, and I get lost in the music. Something weirder happens to me as well. If I am staring at my computer screen, watching the tracks I am recording on my Digital Audio Workstation or even staring at the keys on my synthesizer, my vision drifts.

It's as if my focus goes "beyond" the screen or keys. To understand what I am talking about, hold your finger out in front of your face roughly 10-12 inches away. Stare at your finger, bringing it into focus. Now, look beyond your finger to a wall or a television, whatever is a few feet beyond. Bring that background into focus. You can see how the finger still exists, but it loses visual priority.

This is what happens to me, and I feel as if my senses are heightened, that I am flowing with whatever I am doing, that I am tapping into the zone.

Ironically, this was also discussed in a book series called *Ian Lang's Blueprint for the Mind* series. It's nice to know that I am not the only one who has experienced this, hahaha.

Do not be wary when this happens to you. Now that you have started removing those negative thoughts from your mind and are working toward your goal, you can experience this heightened level of concentration as you rehearse, record, perform. When my focus begins to shift as I am working, I get the same feeling I have when I am in the zone, like the time I performed "Sweating Bullets" or when I break glass on television shows.

Why am I telling you this? Because I want you to experience it, too. Being in the zone is an advanced state of mind, and I believe you'll experience it more naturally and frequently if you figure out what time of day or night is your creative get-up-and-go-moment.

You do this by dedicating a time slot every day to working toward your goal. Is it 5 a.m., before you go to work? Is it right after school at 4 o'clock? Or is it 9 p.m. after the kids settle down for bed? Choose a time and stick to it for one week. At the end of the week, how productive did you feel? It was amazing? Great, keep it up, keep working at the same time.

If you felt really good about what you accomplished during the week but still feel you could have been a little more productive, try a different time of day or night. You can always review your *Mind Over Music* workbook to revisit those amazing times that you were on fire musically. Look for a pattern that involves time. Did those amazing times generally happen at night? Early morning?

PS: I should stop right here and tell you that you CAN be as productive at ANY time of the day. I've performed just as amazingly at 7 a.m. on a television show as I did at 11 p.m. on another show. The purpose of finding a "best time" for your creative juices to flow is because we are creatures of habit. I want you habitually working on your goal, and if it seems you work harder and get more done in the evening, and feel a bit slower in the morning, then so be it. Go with the evening for now.

Creating YOUR Space

Now let's take it even further. If you want those dedicated daily time slots to cruise by full of fire, you also need to establish a "creative space" in your house, whether it's your bedroom, your garage, your basement, or wherever works for you. Every musician needs a creative space. When you have a dedicated space to nurture your musical children, you will feel more inspired and full of the motivational spark of creativity, especially the more time you spend in that dedicated space.

You probably already have a creative space, which is why I didn't cover this first. But it still needs to be brought to your attention just how important it is to have your own home studio (if you plan to record at home) or a basement or garage changed into a rehearsal space for you to work on a song, or even a recording/rehearsal studio nearby that you can visit daily to get you into the flow.

I must deduce that musicians who still feel bored after working through this process are most likely a victim of their surroundings. If you're trying to write a song in the living room while leaning back on the couch with your feet kicked up on the coffee table while the news is on the television, your kids are playing in the background, and your cat keeps jumping on your lap, it can stifle the creativity.

Your creative space should be a place of solace without those everyday distractions. Being in your personal creative space without distractions can stoke those creative flames. When you're tired from a long day and feeling drained and not up to working on your creative goal, just walking into your creative space can help lift your energy.

Even if you walk into your creative space on those rough days and think, "I'm still too tired to work on music tonight," you can still be inspired to create. It's a neat little trick that has worked for me many times. I simply turn on all my equipment, fire up the latest project I am working on, and set an alarm for ten minutes, telling myself, "If in ten minutes I'm still tired, I'll call it a night."

Hahaha, I never call it a night. Once I am ten minutes into a project, I am hooked. It is always enough to get me into the zone, and it can be enough spark to put you in the zone and flip that switch to full-on creative mode, revitalizing your mind and body with ample energy to work on your music.

Bottom line, you need to be in your creative space every day.

You love music, right? Yep, that's what I thought.

So quit avoiding it! Get into your space, live and breathe in your space. Your space is now a part of you! Quit coming up with tedious unrelated tasks like catching up on your favorite Netflix show, just to pull you away from it.

Disabling ALL Distractors

As I just said (and I didn't stutter), once you have your creative space, you live in it and breathe in it and work in it because it is now part of you. It is part of your life, part of what will help you eliminate procrastination and keep you focused on the finish line. Even with your alarm set for 7 p.m., or whatever time you have deemed your get-up-and-go-moment, if you come home early from work one day and have nothing going on, I strongly suggest that you walk into your creative space.

Turn on that equipment just for those ten minutes. This could inspire you to work throughout the day. The "turning on the equipment" tactic is a great inspirer. The next thing you know, your alarm will go off, telling you it is your usual time to work in your creative space. But you've already been in there for the last five hours, and at this rate, you're so on fire, so in flow with the music, so in the zone, that it might be another five hours before you stop!

However, little things can still distract us, even in our creative space. In this day and age, we have TONS of little moments that distract us from our goal. We discussed a few earlier.

For example, my creative space is free of most distractions. There is no television to bug me, my dogs are upstairs, I am not sitting on my rocking chair, which by the way, would make me sleep. So, it is easy to work—except for my cell phone.

As I was writing earlier today, I had a phone call from a neighbor who just wanted to chat. While I am always happy to speak with them, I KNEW I had to focus on writing. However, I answered the phone. Fifteen minutes in, I am up walking all over my house (I tend to walk from room to room when I am on the phone) and we're still chatting.

Then I get another call, from a fellow coach who wanted to run a few things by me. I hung up from my neighbor to take the other call, but now I was completely out of my creative writing flow, pulled away from my creative space to discuss something that, although very important, could have waited until my writing time was over. This was all because I allowed my phone to ring.

After I hung up from the second call, I decided to take my dog outside and then fix myself a quick bite to eat. Another half hour later I finally got back to writing. But instead of going back down to my studio to write in my creative space, I decided to sit upstairs on my lounge chair.

Big mistake. My little chihuahua Taco is head over heels nuts about me. He HAD to sit on my lap. So here I sat, stiffly in a lounge chair with my dog on my lap and my PC on the arm rest, trying to write. All the while, Taco was turning around to stare at me until I pet him ... and pet him ... and pet him some more, hahaha. Soon I became tired, turned off my computer, and took a two-hour nap.

Needless to say, I let these distractions "distract" me from my goal. I am sharing this so that you learn to eliminate distractions from your creative space, so that you don't make my mistakes. When you decide on your time to work on your goal, you must give ALL of yourself to that time. You MUST allot that time slot for your creative space just as if it is a JOB (although one you love.) You MUST be in your studio or rehearsal room working on your intention. And you MUST eliminate any and all distractions from your creative space.

If you have distractions, such as the ringer on your phone, your Facebook text window open on a computer, a television playing in the background, these are annoyances that can pull you away from your goal. The only way to live in the zone is to eliminate these distractions.

So, turn off that phone, put it in airplane mode, turn off the Internet, turn off that television, shut the door to keep the kids, cats, and dogs out, and get to work.

Keeping a Super-Simple Workspace Calendar
Now that you've gotten serious about the work, you've designated a dedicated work time, you have your creative space, and you have eliminated those distractions, it's time to start your super-simple calendar to keep you on point.

For those of you familiar with my books *Unleash Your Creative Mindset*, *Raise Your Voice*, and *SingFit*, you know I am all about keeping track of your progress. I keep a Mindset diary, Ultimate Vocal Workout diary, and SingFit journals.

Don't worry, you won't have to keep a big diary to write out tons and tons of paragraphs like you did in your *Mind Over Music* workbook. I will make it even simpler.

We're going to use a wall calendar. As soon as possible, purchase a physical hold-in-your-hand wall calendar to hang in your creative workspace. It can be a picture calendar with pictures of dachshunds or a beach calendar with palm trees or your favorite sports team, whatever floats your boat. But I will give you bonus point if it's a calendar with music-related pictures, hahaha.

The best calendar is one that has a square for each day of the week, which allows you to write small notes as short as your whisper words in the square with the day's date concerning what you plan to work on for that day. This will look clean and organized, especially if you write your time in the upper left corner of each square.

The moment you start working in your creative space, reach up and write down what time you start. Preferably it is the exact minute your alarm goes off! When that alarm goes off, you need to be in your creative space, ready to roar. Not heading there; you must already be there.

When I worked construction, I was adamant about being right at the toolbox at 7 a.m., not walking from my car to the tool box at 7 a.m. Work time was 7 a.m., not the time we head to our work spot. Many workers didn't like this attitude. They felt that when work starts is when they head to work. That is a negative attitude. We were being paid starting at 7 a.m., not 7:07 when some wandered over to the toolbox.

Your time is the price you're paying for your creativity. So, if you are currently dedicating an hour every day but slowly start wandering down into your basement to your creative space once your alarm goes off, you've lost several precious working minutes. If you develop a sluggish attitude, it could take you another five to ten minutes to grab a bottle of water, hit the restroom, and fire up your equipment before you start your "hour." You could potentially be losing an hour of work per week toward your goal because of your sluggish attitude.

Do not have this attitude! It doesn't cut it! Be ready to work and have your equipment fired up and ready to roar.

If you're concerned by the amount of time you dedicate to work, I'm not going to suggest a general amount of time. That is your call. It is not my responsibility to tell you that you have to work in your creative space for 20 minutes daily, or an hour, or half a day.

The point is, you need to stay the minimum amount of time per day that you know you will focus and work on music. Then you must agree to be in your creative space at the exact minute your alarm goes off, working on something, regardless of whether it is writing a song or recording a guitar track.

Back to your calendar. As soon as you write the time down, also add a short note (remember to make them as short as your whisper words, if possible) that states what you'll be working on for that day. If you are recording vocal parts, add, "Tracking vocals." If you're writing the last chorus of your latest song, add, "Finishing chorus to 'Lisa.'" Whatever your goal for this session in your creative space, write it down.

As you write your notes for that day's task, please visualize what you're going to be tackling that day—and visualize it in high speed. When I visualize working on my task as I write my notes, I like to visualize a wall clock with the minute hand spinning faster than the second hand, while I also see myself accomplishing my task (which might take one or two hours) in only a matter of seconds.

By racing through the task in my mind and seeing the task finished, my motivational spark of creativity has a jumpstart before I even begin.

I should also note that I never visualize where the clock starts or stops. I don't want to implant a specific work time starting and ending because I want my creative flow to be ready to start at any time and work as long as needed.

Generally, time is irrelevant once this becomes routine, because your time will flow. If for some reason you start to feel bored in the middle of a task, check yourself and see what is causing it. Maybe you're tired of working on the bass line. If you're just not feeling it and it isn't attributed to any boredom or fear triggers, hey, we're all human, so every once in a while you can call it a short night. You can stop and shut down the creative space for the day.

OR, if it IS the result of a trigger, such as a boredom trigger, you can switch roles. Jump from working on tracking vocals to recording a bass line, or switch from writing lyrics to going over the chord structure of the song. If at all possible, try to stay stimulated during these times. Seek out the trigger affecting you and switch gears to clear that trigger from your mind.

At the end of your session, write down the time you shut down shop. If you generally go from 7 p.m. to 8 p.m., and that is what you did today, put a dash after your starting time in the upper left-hand corner and add your end time, so it reads, "7-8". And if you do have the occasional off day, don't beat yourself up about it. But you still must write the correct time on your calendar, such as, "7-7:27."

Also review what you've written on your calendar. Take a moment to reflect to see how you feel about what you've accomplished for the day. If you feel you've accomplished what you set out to finish for the day, and you feel good about it, then fine, you're done for the day. If you didn't reach your goal, you might dedicate another 20 to 30 minutes or an hour.

However, if you're on fire when that alarm goes off, don't worry about reflection, just keep going. You might end up working 3-1/2 hours that day before you call it night. In this case, you'd write, "7-10:30."

But wait, there's more. If the motivational spark of creativity had you working all those hours, I am betting you did more than track vocals or finish that one song. This is why I wanted your calendar notes to be short. If you accomplished more work in your creative space than you wrote down on your calendar at start time, add it to your calendar!

Bottom line, keeping track of your time and adding work notes, while always seeing it on a wall calendar every day, will challenge your mind to always go longer.

Once you've honed and developed your creative space work ethic, you'll find that you have more bouts of creative inspiration with physical/mental energy. You can also use whisper words while in your creative space.

Priming Your Mind with Whisper Words

We've already covered whisper words, but here's another spin on how to use them. You should know that you're already priming your mind by listening daily to your Music Caffeine Playlist and panting while thinking of your goal. The act of flooding your mind with high-powered music AND pulling more oxygen into your body AND thinking about your goal is breaking down that connection to procrastination.

It is reprogramming your music DNA to DO something instead of avoiding it. You can also slip in a few whisper words and let them encourage you during your Music Caffeine Playlist sessions. However, these whisper words aren't third person, like our other whisper words. These suggestions are more like typical affirmations:

I am flow.

I am in the zone.

I am a _____ (singer, musician, songwriter).

Yes, we can flow, be in flow, and become the flow all the time. You can tap into a similar experience as the runner's high, experiencing more scenarios where you felt you were in the zone. You can tune in to your musical DNA.

Remember, you are ALWAYS a singer, a musician, a songwriter. But at times, you simply forgot that truth. Being human, we tend to prioritize everything non-music related in our lives as more important because we have been told that we cannot make a living at music. But you CAN make music a major part of your life.

Like Joe says, "Where's the proof? Prove to me you cannot do this!"

What could be more important than living the life that is programmed into your DNA?

You have the tools to bear that child. So let's do it! It isn't enough to dream about it. Work through your *Mind Over Music* workbook and visualize your goal while listening to your Music Caffeine Playlist; you must take steps to accomplish that goal.

You must decide right now that you WILL do something EVERY DAY that benefits and leads you toward finishing your goal. No more excuses, no more laziness, no more accepting your fears when they aren't real. There is no proof they are real. Quit only dreaming the dream and start doing the work.

Working on music is living in the moment. It's allowing you to develop the skills to be in the zone. It is working toward the goal. Don't overthink it. Don't nitpick your creativity during those times. Write a song and move along. Write another song and don't overanalyze it. Let the creativity flow and clean up later.

Craft your song, build your band, whatever your goal, and strive for more with every session in your creative space. Keep writing and rehearsing and recording.

Above all, have fun. Music is meant to be fun. If you have fun, you will successfully accomplish all your goals!

In ending, don't forget that you can never learn enough. You've got to be a student every day, a musician every day, a performer every day, and a songwriter every day. Do things in your "music time" that involve all of these. If you have a humble mind, accepting that you can learn more every day puts you another step closer to your goal!

Chapter Nine
WHERE'S THE PROOF?

THIS BOOK STARTED BECAUSE OF JOE. As you know, I challenged him to write it, but he turned it around on me, hahaha. I am very happy he did. It made me look at my own life, helped me find my fire again. Within that fire, I realized that I do indeed LOVE teaching as much as I love playing music. I thought to myself that I truly wished I was doing something with teaching that also involved playing. Which led me back to the performance workshops.

Oddly enough, when you find your fire and start on that path, many things unfold. One thing that unfolded for me was the job of a touring vocal coach, something I hadn't fully considered, though I had that moment of jealousy over a touring vocal coach that you may recall from early in this book. Well, as things usually unfold, I got an email the day I finished writing the first draft of this book (obviously, I am adding this after the fact) from a company involved with Bollywood in India offering me a job as, you guessed it, a touring vocal coach working with Pritam, India's most renowned and respected music composer, for his US tour featuring a phenomenal group of musicians and well-known singers (Amanat Ali, Nakash Aziz, Sreerama Chandra, Shalmali Kholgade, Amit Mishra, Antara Mitra, and Shilpa Rao.)

I am beyond ecstatic. So, where's the proof you cannot do what you love if you clear the path? There is none! Which brings me to the point of this final chapter. As the story goes, the original plan was for

Joe and me to co-write this book. But as he read it and loved it, he felt it was complete, so he was unsure where he'd fit in. Well, he fits in as the inspiration for this entire process.

We still have ways to share Joe's story, so here are three articles that tie in to Joe's journey from music lover to music performer and recording artist:

OVERCOMING FEAR: HOW I OVERCAME MY FEAR OF SINGING IN PUBLIC

Almost everyone is interested in overcoming fear—or should be. Whether you want to speak in public, open a new business, talk to potential dates, do stand-up comedy, climb a mountain—or *anything* you haven't done before—you're bound to feel fear and want help in overcoming fear.

Well, how do you do it?

After recording six albums of songs, my Band of Legends politely nudged me to perform live. While I've spoken on stage numerous times over the decades, I never *sang* on stage. Thinking about it brought up serious fears. Even terror.

A friend remembers me saying I would NEVER sing in public. I had to overcome panic attacks, anxiety ambushes, and near nervous breakdowns to overcome the fear of public speaking. But public *singing?*

Forget it.

I didn't even sing in the shower. Childhood memories of being humiliated when I tried to speak or sing stayed with me. I overcame the speaking one. But I refused to even touch singing. It felt too vulnerable. I managed to do it in the studio for my six albums, by basically managing my adrenaline, but I couldn't accept ever singing on stage live. No way.

But I did it.

I did it!

And it was a huge success. I was strong and confident, owned the stage, and led my Band of Legends into a triumphant performance. It was a historic moment. It was a personal breakthrough. And it will live forever in my mind as a moment of greatness for me.

So, how did I go from terrified to terrific?

I'll share my own process, as it will illustrate the art of overcoming fear. I'm sure you can be inspired by this adventure. I of course did all the standard things that I teach, from practicing *ho'oponopono* (as I wrote about in my books *Zero Limits* and *AT Zero*) to rehearsing in the studio and in my mind.

But two months before the show, I also—

1. I got coaching.

A basic rule of self-improvement is this:

You can accomplish more if you have someone who believes in you almost more than you believe in yourself.

I first saw that insight in the home of Jerry and Esther Hicks, of Abraham fame, decades ago. Jerry (who has passed on and I greatly miss) told me he first heard it in an early television western. I don't recall the name of the show, but I do remember the impact the principle had on me.

I started Miracles Coaching more than a decade ago for that reason—to give people someone who could believe in them. To help them overcome fear. To help them attract miracles. I've had a lot of people support me and coach me in performing:

Jen Sincero is a badass author of two *New York Times* bestselling books, *You Are a Badass* and the recent *You Are a Badass at Making Money*. I discovered her first book years ago, knew it would be a hit, and interviewed her. We stayed in touch.

I had lunch with Jen when she came to Austin for a book signing. I knew she had been in a band at one point, so I told her my dilemma. She told me that I had already done the hard part of singing.

"You sang for Melissa Etheridge," she explained, referring to when I had a private songwriting lesson with the rock icon last November. "Singing one on one is harder than singing on stage, and you sang for an icon you idolize and adore."

The last time I saw Melissa Etheridge, just for a moment after her show in San Antonio in June, she told me she loves my latest album, *The Great Something*. She said to "keep at it."

I dedicated that album to her. There's a song on it I wrote for her. Her encouragement helped me stay motivated. She once told me, "Feel the fear and do it anyway."

Sarah McSweeney is a singer-songwriter who is on my first album, *Blue Healer*. She was the first person I sang for. We met and she told me she always feels nervous before getting on stage. But she thinks of herself as a messenger, not a singer. That reframe made the idea of singing easier. "I am a messenger," she said. "I focus on the song's message."

That insight helped me drop the idea of being a singer and adopt the idea of being a messenger. It helped me relax a little.

Meghan Sandau is a new friend. She has promoted big music events. She wanted to see me do a concert. She said she likes my music. Her belief in me helped make me more secure. In fact, none of this would happen without her.

She set up the event for my Band of Legends to perform. She held my hand and encouraged me. Meghan also suggested I do an energy-clearing session with Nicole Pigeault of Los Angeles. I love energy work and do clearings for others, so I leaped at the chance to hire Nicole. Turned out to be one of the most powerful esoteric washes ever. The hour session helped me release fears and settle into confidence.

But she wasn't the only person to support me. Guitar Monk Mathew Dixon has been coaching me for years now. We've made numerous instrumental albums together, such as *Invoking Divinity*. He stayed in my corner, listening to me rehearse, listening to me confide my fears, and urging me to hang in there.

Then there's Patrick Stark in Canada. He's a filmmaker making a movie about overcoming fear.

It's called "One Life: No Regrets." He interviewed me for it. He plans to sing onstage with the band U2. But it will be the first time he'll sing on stage EVER.

Imagine it. The first time you sing in public anywhere is on stage with U2 and thousands watching. Well, if Patrick can drum up that kind of courage, then so can I. Right?

I found preparing for the event mainly a battle with my mind. Most of my thinking was negative. It was all, "What if it goes bad?" But Mindy Audlin came to visit. She teaches what if *up* thinking. She wrote the book *What If It All Goes Right?* She coached me in other ways to think: What if it is a breeze? What if I love it? It also helps to see people successful in one field try their hand in a completely different field.

James Altucher tried stand-up comedy. He's a writer. He's doing something out of his comfort zone. But he's willing to do it for the experience, and he's sharing his learning curve to inspire others. Though I haven't met him, knowing he was stepping out beyond his fear fortified me to do it, too.

Of course, my beautiful Nerissa believed in me, too. She and I practiced "The Remembering Process" that Daniel Barrett taught me. We talked about the live show as if it had happened in the past and we were remembering how great it went. (See the book Daniel and I wrote: *The Remembering Process*.) So the first thing I did was gather people who could coach and inspire me.

Next—

2. I got educated.

To prepare for my show, I attended an online Masterclass with David Mamet and another with Usher. Both were astoundingly good.

Mamet is a Pulitzer Prize-winning playwright and screenwriter. I think he is a genius. He said most people are afraid to be bad to be good. You have to be bad first to start being good.

You have to start *someplace*. I reminded myself of this as I prepared for the live event.

While I wanted to step out on stage and be "perfect," Mamet reminded me that I will probably step out and be bad. But bad is where you start. You can't get to great without starting at bad. Usher said to prepare, to be confident, but to expect something to go wrong.

Don't expect perfection.

He told a story of a performance where he injured himself at the beginning of a two-hour show and had to keep dancing and singing despite the pain. His insights and pointers were priceless in helping me create a mindset for success.

And I bought a set of audios called *The Relaxed Musician*. It's a 14-day course in exploring limiting beliefs. It helped me realize I had a big belief that if I looked bad as a performer, it would hurt my reputation in other areas, such as an author or speaker. But like most beliefs, it didn't hold up.

I could forget all my lyrics and totally wash out on stage and it wouldn't even dent my image anywhere else. Most people forgive and forget. In fact, a miss on stage could give me a terrific story about how I bombed and lived.

But I didn't stop there.

I read a terrific book on how to deliver an unforgettable live performance. I liked the book so much, I read it twice. It was called *The Musician's Guide to a Great Live Performance*. It became my bible. I read it on planes, took it with me on my iPad, and shared it with singer-songwriter friends.

And I read a wonderful book on overcoming fear and panic titled *You 1, Anxiety 0*. Author Jodi Aman helped take the mask off of fear so I could see what it really was: an illusion. I soaked up the wisdom in this book. It really helped me.

I also read a 1950 book by Vernon Howard called *Word Power*. It was about how you talk to yourself, as well as to others, affects your behavior and your results. It's not so much affirmations but self-talk. Pretending you are fearless by saying "I am a fearless performer" is a way to begin *being* a fearless performer.

And I read a recent book called *Succeed*. It explained that just visualizing success is a plan for failure *unless* you also visualize planning for setbacks. In other words, thinking the show will go without a flaw is not realistic, as Usher pointed out. There is no such thing as perfection.

But visualizing success and understanding there is work to do to get there can almost guarantee the result you want. That was a mind-spinning insight.

I did more, too—

3. I got Nevillized.

With Meghan's urging, I wrote out a script of how I wanted the show to go. I focused on my feelings, not anyone else's, so I could focus on what I could control. The script was a type of Nevillizing (which I write about in my book *The Attractor Factor*): feeling as if the event *already* happened and happened the way I envisioned it.

I didn't visualize the show happening, I visualized that the show *already* happened. Big difference. I wrote the script from the point of view of the next day, *after* I performed on stage.

I read and re-read it every day for a week before the show.

And—

4. I got relaxed.

I got massages, I got plenty of rest, I drank lots of water, and I went into a flotation tank at The Zero Gravity Institute for 90 minutes the day before the show. I was doing whatever I could to be at peak form when I stepped onstage. I was taking care of my body and mind. I was getting ready for my moment.

5. I got faith.

Faith doesn't always mean something religious. Faith in yourself, faith in other people, faith in my practice and prep, faith in my Band of Legends—all of it gives a level of confidence that allows the best to surface. As a slogan I coined says, "It is what you accept." I accepted that the moment would be perfect, even in any imperfections. It would be "perfectly imperfect."

I let go. I trusted. And, after two months of preparing, what happened?

My Band of Legends and I performed on July 21st at The Townsend in Austin. I'm the luckiest musician alive to have a band of this caliber: drummer Joe Vitale (yes, same name as mine), bass man Glenn Fukunaga, and lead guitarist Daniel Barrett.

These incredible musicians encouraged me, supported me, and brought my songs to life.

We raised the roof and tore down the walls.

We shook the earth and wowed the crowd.

Talk about overcoming fear!!!

I gave everything I had in me, delivering my messages with energy, enthusiasm, electricity, and a sense of fearlessness and fun. At the end of our set, we got a standing ovation.

A standing ovation!

I did it. And I *loved* it! Now, what do you fear that is time for you to do? Isn't today a good day to begin overcoming fear?

Expect miracles.

Ao Akua
Joe

THE FIFTH MIRACLE: HOW I CREATED AN ALBUM FROM SCRATCH WHEN I THOUGHT I WAS BONE DRY

It was October of 2012 that I told my music producer and friend, Daniel Barrett, that my desire to make more music was dead. I didn't feel inspired or connected to the muse. I was happy with the four albums of healing music I had already created, but I didn't see any more on the horizon.

I felt done.

As we talked, I had a sneaking suspicion that I may be deceiving myself. After all, self-sabotage is rampant in virtually each of us, and we usually don't even know we are doing it.

Was I?

Daniel suggested we find a way to ramp up my energy for music. He didn't know how, but he felt there was a solution.

"I know how," I told him. I did, too.

I knew a way to jump-start the muse, but I wasn't sure I wanted to do it. He asked me to explain.

I took a deep breath and said, "I can set the intention to record five new songs by Christmas."

Christmas was only two months away. It would be a miracle to write and record five new songs by then—especially starting from zero—and certainly after exhausting myself having *just* completed my fourth album, *The Healing Song*.

Daniel didn't miss a beat. "Why not go for ten songs?"

That made me gasp. It would be raising the bar even for me. I had already broken records by creating four albums in less than two years. Four miracles were plenty. But I accepted the challenge. We agreed that I would strive to create ten original songs within two months, and together we would record them to create my fifth album. We both felt the exhilarating energy of having a goal that scared us and yet delighted us. We both felt expectant, uncertain, open, and willing. But we had *no idea* how a new album would come out of nothing.

Now here's where the story gets *really* interesting …

Remember, I didn't have *any* ideas for new songs or *any* passion for new music. I felt tapped out. Yet the new intention "called forth" more music. The new goal stirred my creative self. Within days I had new songs coming to me. Within weeks I had almost two dozen ideas.

I couldn't turn off the creative juices!

I would be sitting, reading a book on my iPad, and suddenly a song idea would enter my consciousness. I was smart enough to stop everything and write it down. (Always take action, remember.)

Other times I felt inspired to check out early or vintage rock 'n' roll, what's called rockabilly music. I simply followed the muse to see what occurred. I loved the searching, exploring, and learning. (Always follow inspiration, too.)

Within weeks I had over two dozen pretty good songs. From those, I picked nine that I thought were solid. I left a tenth idea open to inspirational improvisation in the studio. I felt ready to record album number five!

My band—not really "mine," but they were the same musicians who recorded *Strut!* and *The Healing Song* with me—got together again. We went into the studio on December 18th and 19th—right before Christmas, you'll note—and recorded ten new tracks.

I'm told music doesn't usually come together this quickly, or easily, or with this much energy and focus. But we got together in the studio and made space for magic to happen around my songs.

The result is my fifth music album, titled *Sun Will Rise*. And it feels like another miracle.

When I held the finished audio CD in my hands and listened to the original music I wrote and performed, brought to life with the musicians who supported me, I started to cry. To think that this was created out of "thin air" is astonishing. To think that the songs are so good and the music so amazing and the messages so relevant, just makes me stop and stare in awe and gratitude. I am grateful beyond belief. It's yet another miracle.

Miracles are indeed happening all the time. This story is living proof of it. And it all begins with an intention.

In case you are curious, here are the stories behind each track on *Sun Will Rise* from healingrockmusic.com:

"You Gotta!" is self-help rock 'n' roll. It's fun, upbeat, and carries the message that "you gotta" take action. Since I'm a big proponent of action, this song and its message felt like the right lead for the new album. Thanks to "my band"—drummer Joe Vitale, bass player Glenn Fukunaga, lead guitarist Daniel Barrett—this song opens with a "you gotta dance to this" feel. Add saxophone by Greg Williams and this one is irresistibly delicious! You gotta hear it!

"Sun Will Rise" came to me "out of the blue" as I held a guitar and just started to sing what came into my being. When I first played it for Daniel, he was speechless. He said it had the potential to be a radio hit. My staff says my message to the world is to have faith, that the "sun will rise" again. Your current reality is just that—current. It'll change. The sun *will* rise again. This song is your reminder.

"The Secret" isn't based on the movie I was in of the same name. Instead, it was prompted by a haunting song by Leonard Cohen. His song had the hypnotic refrain "Everybody knows ..." but his lyrics were negative. His dark song is a great one to commit suicide to. I wanted something hypnotic but with a positive message. I wanted something healing. The result is what I call "The Secret" and *you know* it will do you good to listen to it.

"Sperichil" is rockabilly music. It's pure fun. No special message in the lyrics, but the voice and the vibe are all about *be happy now!* The name is simply the early spelling of the word "spiritual." I surprised myself recording this song as I spontaneously howled like a wolf during parts of it. There is a happy contagiousness to this track that simply makes me smile and feel good. Isn't that what life is all about? Isn't that healing music? Be happy now. Smile! Dance! Love!

"Expectations" is a hypnotic intermission where I played a special double-neck guitar, where the top is a regular guitar and the bottom is a baritone guitar. With the professionals behind me on this one, the result is something I could listen to all day long. When I first heard it in the studio, I said, "Call this one *Expectations*, because it suggests something is about to happen, but you don't know what." You are free to expect whatever you want, positive or negative, and this music helps you feel the moment. Talk about healing!

"My Electric Car" is about my relationship to my electric car (which I've written about on this blog before). I love this song because of the lyrics and the blues rock music the band came up with. I really believe this one could become a gas guzzler's anthem. You gotta hear it. There are moments in this track that send shivers of joy up my spine. It's an example of how music becomes magic. Whew!

"Train of Women" is a rock ballad about a man who faces his fears and falls in love. It's about one hundred and fifty women, all wearing bikinis, who come to see him. He is at first afraid, asking for everything from a crocodile to a bodyguard to being taken to Area 51, but by the end he falls in love. The old saying is true, what looks like your demon is really your angel in disguise. This song is fun, fast, funny, and more. Call it a Rorschach test song. Whatever you get from it is what you get from it. It's a mirror. It's "Healing Music" at its best. Rock on!

"Isaac the Psychic" is my attempt to create a Shel Silverstein–Johnny Cash "Boy Named Sue" kind of song. I came up with a character and a story and a funny chorus and wove it into a song. My band—the experts that they are—created a reggae upbeat rhythm, and the whole thing came together. It's funny and memorable. You'll smile listening to it. After all, I'm so psychic, I know you're reading this.

"Super Heroes" came to me after my guitar teacher, Matthew Dixon, taught me a new chord progression. I wrote words to that progression. Since I had just met actor/bodybuilder/Hulk Lou Ferrigno and actor/Superman Dean Cain, I turned the song into messages from their characters. This is another feel good, relaxing song. It could be the theme to a television show. It's about *you* being the new superhero. Don't wait for a hero. *Be one* now.

"Ti Amo" was written for my love, Nerissa. I felt the urge to write a love song and thought, what better way to do it than to think of who I love and just write a song for her. I did. I believe anyone can feel the love in this one. Nerissa says she does. Love heals.

All of the above is a reminder that miracles are possible for all of us. Yes, even you.

I created this fifth album of healing songs by declaring an intention. I didn't have any reason or motivation or evidence that I could write ten new (and good, IMHO) songs in two months. But declaring an intention "called forth" all this music. You can do this, too.

What do you want to attract? What do you want to "call forth"? What miracle would be cool to experience? Declare it.

Ao Akua
Joe

THE GREAT SOMETHING: CREATING MY SIXTH SINGER-SONGWRITER ALBUM WITH LESSONS FROM MELISSA ETHERIDGE

I'm going to share a hot-off-the-press story with you here. Then we can look at how to apply the principles in it to your life. Ready?

I just finished recording my sixth singer-songwriter album. It's called *The Great Something*. I dedicated my new singer-songwriter album to the great Melissa Etheridge.

While the previous five albums all reveal a musician growing in confidence and ability, each one better than the last, this latest one broke all boundaries. The songs are better than ever. The singing is hands down the best ever. The music is stellar, going from swing to ballad to rock to (as my drummer put it) "improvised symphony of genius."

Why is this album so much better than all the others? What happened?

I used everything I teach about self-help, goal-setting, and manifestation to create this album, from setting a clear intention to gathering my Band of Legends to taking action on the ideas and opportunities that arose as I moved toward the recording date.

While all these elements are part of what make The Law of Attraction work in your favor, clearly the biggest turning point for me was attracting my private two-hour songwriting lesson with rock icon, Melissa Etheridge. I've already written four blog posts about my time with her. (See PS below for links to those "Attracting Melissa Etheridge" articles.) I won't repeat myself (much) here, but I openly declare that my time with Melissa deeply influenced this entire album. In fact, I've dedicated it to her. Let me explain:

First, I used some of her music dynamics to create new songs.
The song "Melissa Said" is, as my producer called it, "The greatest thank you card of all time." It's an original song I wrote for Melissa, using some of the arrangements she shared with me about making music. My band got goosebumps listening to my homage to Melissa. It is stellar. It is three minutes of gratitude. (Wait till Melissa hears it!)

Second, the title track song was directly influenced by my time with Melissa.
While Melissa was too wise to tell me what to do, her feedback helped me learn lessons for myself. It was the Socratic Method. Socrates didn't give you the answer. He helped you think of it on your own. Being with Melissa helped me realize the title track song (and the album) needed to be called *The Great Something*, my phrase for God or the Divine. (It was originally going to be called *The Miracle*.) That insight redirected the entire album.

Third, and more importantly, Melissa urged me to write from the first person.
"The Great Something," the title track song, is raw. It's from my view of life, my hard times, and my discovery of The Great Something. The band was blown away with the power and depth of it. It is riveting. It is revealing. That is a direct result of taking to heart what Melissa told me about writing in the first person.

Fourth, when I was with Melissa, I shared the opening lines of a song that had come to me in my sleep.
Melissa liked what she heard. Because of that, I felt encouraged to complete the song. I did. It is the most hauntingly beautiful thing I've ever penned. It's called "Hey You," and it's designed to heal any hurting heart. Guitar Monk Matthew Dixon added his sweet guitar on it, and it is deliciously healing.

Fifth, Melissa taught me to feel my message when I sang.
As a result, my singing on a singer-songwriter ballad I wrote was, as my producer called it, "Sinatra-est." It was probably the highest compliment he could give me. My voice compared even remotely to Frank Sinatra's was enough to make me speechless. I just followed what Melissa taught me and *felt* the song as I sang it.

Obviously, I absorbed Melissa's wisdom and vibe and infused it into this new album. Before it was released, I had big dreams for this new album. As Daniel Barrett, producer (and coauthor of the book *The Remembering Process*), told me, "You can't think average thoughts and expect extraordinary results."

So, I thought BIG. And it worked!!! The album turned out great!!!

This post isn't about getting you to buy the album. Instead, I'm sharing all of this with you to demonstrate how the Law of Attraction, magic, and miracles work.

Here's a quick recap:
1. I set an intention to create a new album that surpassed all my others.
2. I visualized and felt the end-result already done and a mega success.
3. I cleared any limiting beliefs along the way, freeing me to be my best.
4. I took action by writing songs, gathering my band, booking the studio.

5. I seized opportunities, such as grabbing my music lesson with Melissa.
6. I let go and went with the flow, while keeping my intention in mind.

I'm sure you can do this, too. You have a dream, don't you? You could set an intention for it, gather allies, and start to move toward it, right? Are there any real excuses or limitations for doing what you really want to do, if you *really* want to do it? Isn't today a good day to begin? *The Great Something* says YES!

Ao Akua,
Joe

ON WITH THE SHOW

THERE YOU HAVE IT, a super simple way to get back into the zone, light that fire, and succeed!

Now it's time to press on with the show, for YOU to start the show!!! Get started today, not next Monday, or the first day of the New Year, but TODAY.

To recap, it's simple to get you back on track:

1. Start your *Mind Over Music* workbook! Review your life to find those creative sparks and discover what triggers your boredom and fears.
2. Make a decision to set a goal based on what you want to do with music. Set the intention to reach that goal by the deadline you set.
3. Make that Music Caffeine Playlist!
4. Eliminate those triggers! Ask yourself, "Where's the proof?" Use whisper words to overcome your fear triggers and to prime your mind!
5. Set up your creative space and a daily time to work in your creative space!
6. Keep a super simple calendar to keep track of your time and daily projects in your creative space!
7. Become a student every single day and be the artist you are! Never ever stop studying music. You can always learn more about singing, playing, performing, and recording to make you a better musician!

Wait, what? Seven steps? What happened to just three?

Hahaha, it still is three steps, at its core.

If you follow this approach, you will learn to feel that musical fire burn within you every time you practice, every time you write a song, every time you perform. That's when you'll find yourself releasing more music than you ever imagined, playing more gigs than you ever imagined, having those moments of being in the zone more times than you ever imagined.

Do you want to be a star? Well, who doesn't? If it is important enough to you, you will find a way. If it is not, you'll find an excuse.

Do you believe that music is in your DNA?

Prove it!

I KNOW you can prove it!!!

See you at the top!

—JOE AND JAIME

ABOUT JAIME VENDERA

JAIME VENDERA is the author of dozens of books, audio programs, and video training programs, including *Raise Your Voice, Unleash Your Creative Mindset, SingFit, The Ultimate Breathing Workout, The Extreme Scream* audio series, *and The Beyond the Voice* video series. He is also the first documented singer on film to shatter a glass by the power of his voice alone, as seen on over 60 television shows worldwide, including, MythBusters, Dr. Oz, The Truth (UpRoxx), and Superhuman Showdown.

He is also a highly sought-after vocal coach, having an uncanny ability to help singers build and release more range, power, and stamina than ever thought possible. Some of his clients have included singers from the bands Dream Theater, Starset, Skyharbor, Gotthard, Hinder, Thriving Ivory, and many more touring and recording stars. He also teaches these same methods he developed for more vocal range, power, projection, and stamina through his online school, Vendera Vocal Academy. He lives with his wife, Diane, in Ohio.

Jaime can be contacted at http://www.JaimeVendera.com

For more information about the Vendera Vocal Academy, see, http://www.venderavocalacademy.com/join

Follow Jaime Vendera:

Twitter: https://twitter.com/jaimevendera
Instagram: https://www.instagram.com/jaimevendera/
Facebook: https://www.facebook.com/thejaimevendera
YouTube: https://www.youtube.com/user/venderaj
Soundcloud: https://soundcloud.com/vssounds

ABOUT DR. JOE VITALE

DR. JOE VITALE—once homeless but now a motivating *inspirator* known to his millions of fans as "Mr. Fire!"—is the globally famous author of numerous best-selling books, such as *The Miracle, The Attractor Factor, Zero Limits, Life's Missing Instruction Manual, The Secret Prayer, The Awakened Millionaire,* and *Attract Money Now* (free at http://www.AttractMoneyNow.com.)

He is a star in the blockbuster movie *The Secret*, as well as a dozen other films. He has recorded many best-selling audio programs, from *The Missing Secret* to *The Zero Point*. He's also a self-help singer-songwriter, with fifteen albums out and many of his songs nominated for the Posi Award (considered the Grammy's of positive music).

He created Miracles Coaching®, The Awakening Course, The Secret Mirror, Hypnotic Writing, The Awakened Millionaire Academy, and many more life transforming products and services. He lives outside of Austin, Texas with his wife, Nerissa and their pets.

His main website is http://www.JoeVitale.com

For more information about Miracles Coaching® see http://www.MiraclesCoaching.com

Follow Dr. Joe Vitale:

Twitter: https://twitter.com/mrfire
Instagram: https://www.instagram.com/drjoevitale/
Facebook: https://www.facebook.com/drjoevitale
Blog: http://blog.mrfire.com/

www.ingramcontent.com/pod-product-compliance
Lightning Source LLC
Chambersburg PA
CBHW062116080426
42734CB00012B/2890